FROM THE CURSE
of WILLIE LYNCH
to the
NEW AFRICAN AMERICAN GENERATION

Tell Martin that we fulfilled his dream—we got to
the Promised Land. Now we must begin to build
the society that we can all be proud of in Our
Shining City on the Hill.

James C. Rollins

Order this book online at www.trafford.com
or email orders@trafford.com

Most Trafford titles are also available at major online book retailers.

Printed in the United States of America.

ISBN: 978-1-4669-9231-3 (sc)
ISBN: 978-1-4669-9230-6 (e)

Trafford rev. 05/15/2013

 www.trafford.com

North America & international
toll-free: 1 888 232 4444 (USA & Canada)
fax: 812 355 4082

TABLE OF CONTENTS

Acknowledgment

This book could not have been written without the wonderful support of our friends and family. We would also like to thank Kim Hicks for acting as editor throughout this process.

I, Brandy Hicks, would like to thank my grandfather, James C. Rollins, for providing me with this amazing opportunity. I am forever grateful . . .

Introduction

FORTY YEARS OF WANDERING
IN THE WILDERNESS TO THE PROMISED LAND

For forty years, after the death of Martin Luther King, Jr., African Americans wandered in the wilderness of American society as a result of the three hundred year exodus from slavery. For forty years, as with the Jews' exodus from Egypt, African Americans struggled to find their identity, moral center and sense of self worth.

The start of the forty year journey began with the assassination of Dr. Martin Luther King, Jr. in 1968 and ended with the election of President Barack Obama in 2008. During that particular journey, we spent much of the forty years trying to deprogram ourselves from mental slavery; which included planned family destruction, premeditated drug addiction and the de-education of generations through a grossly inferior education system. Other strategies such as economic destruction through financially predatory programs and the use of daily propaganda to destroy any sense of self worth also proved to be triumphant in propelling the mental slavery agenda.

The voyage began with the following speech, given on April 3, 1968, by Dr. Martin Luther King, Jr. The Dr. King speech was delivered on the night before a planned march to the Memphis,

Tennessee sanitation workers who were on strike. The following is an edited version:

> *"I've been to the mountain top. And I've looked over. And I've seen the Promised Land. I may not get there with you, yet we, as a people will get to the Promised Land."*

Americans needed to rediscover who we were; what made us special and recommit ourselves to those values that once helped us to survive for more than three hundred years in the United States of America.

In recent years, we have become more educated, prosperous and morally focused; although the journey is on-going. Still, the road will be hard and long but we see hope in the present and shall continue to see hope in the future. The election of President Barack Obama gave African Americans a sense of hope; we started to believe in ourselves and in turn realize the dream of Dr. King—"that we, as people, will get to the Promised Land."

The Curse of Willie Lynch pointed out the historical mental conditioning and acquired behaviors designed to prevent us from ever realizing our potential as a human race. Today, I am encouraged by the new generation of black children and although it took merely forty The significance of the above speech was that it was a precursor of the long hard and frustrating journey upon which African Americans were about to embark. African years to discover our worth, we know and trust that if we "refuse to let anyone turn us around" we will get to that shining city on the hill; the promised land.

But first, we must educate and empower ourselves through an appreciation of our true economic worth. Second, we must understand that we have the power to significantly impact the politics in the country with our vote. Finally, we must build a moral foundation for future generations to ensure that they will never again have to experience what earlier generations had to endure. In order to do that, we must first try to gain an understanding of our history as African Americans. Who were the African Americans in our history? Who are the African Americans in our present? Who will be there in our future? Why do we have so many problems trying to identify who we are? To begin to solve that problem, we must understand our American history. My quest began with the Million Man March.

On October 16, 1995, a million black men–sons, brother, husbands and fathers made a commitment to themselves to not shirk their duties as fathers to their children and loving husbands to their wives. We conducted a serious examination of our place in the world. It was towering tribute to the spirit, strength, diversity and vision of the "Black man" in America.

We left knowing that the power to transform ourselves was within our individual selves. The bonding signified a collective movement, not driven by the dictates of political structure but by the inner strength and spirits of African Americans. The Million Man March caught many people by surprise, including a reporter from Channel 4 news in Washington, DC who told the world, "There was no fighting or cracking smoking. Yes, no pimping either".

To quote Minister Louis Farrakhan, "The Million Man March, in 1995, was a modern-day miracle called at a time when Black male emasculation was at its peak . . . negative imagery on all fronts, from the death and destruction that stemmed from gang violence to the denigration of Black women, which caused the "Waiting to Exhale" movement of Black male-female separation as Black women went in search of one "good BMW" (black man working).

This stigmatization was caused by the rise in Black male unemployment that was coincidental to a paralleled rise in Black female employment, causing conflict between Black men and women that was fostering more by social engineering than societal circumstance."

It was on this day, in a speech by Minister Farrakhan of the Nation of Islam that I first heard about Willie Lynch. There was something about that part of his message that has resonated with me for the past ten years. It was an explanation as to why we never seem to be able to realize our real potential as black men and women due to gender conflict.

I have always been a firm believer in actually recognizing a problem before being able to determine its solution; we must know what the problems are and why they exist. To this day, I strongly believe that we, as a race, have not come to grips with the problems of our predecessors. There has always been a belief that our problem was "the white man". We have never looked to ourselves as being the problem, when in fact we are the problem.

It has always been my opinion that African Americans were, in some ways self destructive, and until the Farrakhan speech, I never had a place to start to validate that opinion. It was unreasonable, for some, to think that we were the product of a diabolical social engineering strategy. After the Farrakhan speech, I had a platform on which to support that premise, The Willie Lynch legacy.

The African American behavior mentioned in Farrakhan's speech was awfully familiar to me. There had to be an explanation as to why we depend on others for our survival, and in turn blame them when we fail.

Scholars would say that it is too simplistic to attribute our failings to one person—one plan—one scheme, Willie Lynch. We are not that naïve . . . or are we? If true, his efforts at social engineering took place over three hundred years ago. Sometimes it is just as important that a theory is proven wrong just to remove it as a factor for consideration.

In my first book, *The Curse of Willie Lynch*, I attempted to explain the negative impacts of social engineering on African Americans. I also made recommendations which I believe could begin to eliminate those negative impacts.

I started with the history of huge potential, lost opportunities, and squandered resources by African Americans. This is a proud and profound history that very few are aware of today. This history tells of a structured, disciplined society that if allowed to grow and flourish, would have been competitive on a world class level. A history that included elected Congressional Senators and Congressmen; a structured educational system which included some of the same colleges and universities that exist today, banking institutions, and a healthcare system, all post Civil War.

It would be redundant for me to restate all the trials and tribulations of African Americans that have already been well documented. So I will not.

My objective is to expound on the non-sprouted seeds of our society that we never protected or nourished; seeds that should have grown into productive fruits, providing us with an enhanced economic and social status in today's world.

I want to tell my readers how the cornerstone of black society has been eroded to the point of despair, the mindset that caused it, and some possible basic solutions. A viable family is what prevents us from becoming a unequal group of amoral individuals with a conflicted value system, few dreams, and little ambition. Without a strong family, there cannot be a strong society.

The educational system should be the easiest to repair. We must stop placing children in poor learning environments and leaving them there to fail. We have choices and we must exercise those choices. As parents, active involvement is crucial if we want our children to succeed.

The economic wealth of African Americans is larger than most countries in the world today; yet we fail to benefit from that wealth. Instead, we are "Bling-Bling Broke".

In the past we've sent preachers to congress to compete with lawyers, the result was that we received no significant benefit from our congressional representation. African Americans are the second largest voting bloc in the country, yet we have marginalized ourselves by voting for anyone who will promise us civil rights. It seems that we are preconditioned to vote for the Democratic Party. They do not deliver, yet we continue to vote the same way each election. We elect and re-elect Democratic representatives and do not hold them accountable when they fail to deliver on their promises.

Is the American news media responsible for the negative image of African Americans seen around the world? The media has proven to be the most effective instrument of the Willie Lynch Social Engineering Experiment by continuing to project negative, vile images of African Americans on a daily basis for the world to see. More often than not, we are portrayed as being promiscuous, lazy, violent, and ignorant! We are rarely depicted in a positive light.

From the days of slavery, the church has played a pivotal role in black society. Today, more than ever, it is essential that the church play an even more vital role in rebuilding the moral foundation necessary for African American society to grow strong and change. President George W. Bush attempted to support the role of the church through his Faith Based Initiative legislation. This program would have provided financial resources to churches for social programs e.g., daycare in support of job training, drug rehabilitation programs, family counseling, and emergency housing. Most African Americans did not support the initiative because they believed it was a political swindle if it came from President Bush.

The Willie Lynch curse is the one consistent thread that seems to have an affect all African Americans. A majority of African Americans continue to depend on the white-dominated economic and social structure to take care of us, protect us, educate our children, and employ us. In that trust we have forfeited our ability to grow as a race. In 2013 we continue to exhibit social behavior reminiscent of the Willie Lynch Curse.

1

THE CURSE OF WILLIE LYNCH
THE WILLIE LYNCH LEGACY

William Lynch was a white slave owner from Barbados. In 1712, he gave a speech to a number of white slave-owners in the Southern U.S. His diabolical plot to destroy the minds, bodies, souls and spirits of Blacks continues to this very day.

"Gentlemen, I greet you here on the bank of the James River, in the year of our Lord one thousand seven hundred and twelve. First, I shall thank you, the gentlemen of the Colony of Virginia, for bringing me here. I am here to help you solve some of your problems with your slaves. Your invitation reached me on my modest plantation in the West Indies, where I have experimented with some of the newest and still the oldest methods for control of slaves. Ancient Rome would envy us if my program is implemented. As our boat sailed south on the James River, named for our illustrious King, whose version of the Bible we cherish, I saw enough to know that your problem is not unique.

While Rome used cords of wood crosses for standing human bodies along its highways in great numbers, you are here using the tree and rope on occasion. I caught the whiff of a dead slave hanging from a tree a couple miles back. You are not only losing valuable stock by hangings, you are having uprisings, and slaves are running away, your crops are sometimes left in the fields too long for maximum profit, you suffer occasional fires, and your animals are killed.

Gentlemen, you know what your problems are; I do not need to enumerate your problems. I am here to introduce you to a method of solving them. In my bag here, I have a fool proof method for controlling your black slaves. I guarantee every one of you that if installed correctly, you will be able to control your slaves for years. My method is simple. Any member of your family or your overseer can use it.

I have outlined a number of differences among the slaves, and I take these differences and make them bigger. I use distrust and envy for control purposes. These methods have worked on my modest plantation in the West Indies and it will work throughout the South. Take this simple little list of differences, and think about them. On the top of my list is age, but it is there only because it starts with "A", the second is color or shade, there is intelligence, size, sex, size of plantations, attitude of owners, whether the slaves live in the valley, on a hill, east, west, north, south, have fine hair, or is tall or short.

Now that you have a list of differences, I shall give you an outline of action, but before that, I shall assure you that distrust is stronger than trust, and envy is stronger than adulation, respect, or admiration. The Black slave after receiving this introduction shall carry on and will become self refueling and self-generating for hundreds of years, maybe thousands.

Don't forget you must pitch the old Black male vs. the young Black male, and the young Black male vs. the old Black male.

You must use the dark skin vs. the light skin slaves, and the light skin slaves vs. the dark skin slaves. and depend on us. They must love, respect and trust only us. Gentlemen, these kits are you keys to control. Use them. Have your wives and children You must use the female slave vs. the male, and the male vs. the female. You must also have your white servants and overseers distrust all Blacks, but it is necessary that your slaves trust use them, never miss an opportunity, used intensely for one year, the slaves themselves will rein perpetually distrustful.

Thank you gentlemen,
Willie Lynch"

Some say the Willie Lynch speech is a myth or urban legend, while others believe it is factual. Some say that it might be rooted in fact. Let's, for our purposes, lets say that it may be a good place to start to try to understand the strange, self destructive, low self esteem, dependent personality traits that African Americans constantly exhibit. There are periods in our history when we show signs of breaking the Willie Lynch curse, "only to have certain events stop the march to true freedom." One such time occurred after the Civil War, in the form of the BLACK CODES.

During the run-up to the Civil War, the North recruited and trained black men to lead black soldiers in combat against the South. The seeds of a leadership class had begun to be established. These men were educated soldiers with planning and organizing skills, who learned to skillfully lead men in combat. Yet they would not fight to defend their newly won freedoms after the war. This was the foundation for the newly freed slaves to thrive and prosper. This progress stopped, something had changed.

After the Civil War, history established that there was an organized, systematic culling of the black leadership class through murder, and intimidation. There were political and legal structures instituted to scale back the progress of the newly freed slaves i.e., The Black Codes. The purpose was to reduce free blacks to a new kind of legal servitude distinguished by all the disadvantages of slavery and none of its advantages—a state, many argued, that was worse than slavery itself.

Later in our history there was a large scale introduction of drugs in the black community during the Civil Rights Movement of 1960s, and finally the Welfare system—both, the assassins of dreams.

Each of these predatory events was successful because of the Willie Lynch mindset that said, "IT IS NECESSARY THAT YOUR SLAVES TRUST AND DEPEND ON US. THEY MUST LOVE, RESPECT AND TRUST ONLY US."

The end result is African Americans would not financially support themselves in the richest economy in the world. They would make excuses for the catastrophic educational failures of its young in a country that has the best educational system in the world. African Americans are fourteen percent of the population, yet we do not control a proportional amount of the political power, influence or wealth.

The institutions that we look to for building of our moral foundation, the churches, largely have failed us. Some would argue that it is too simplistic to attribute all of these failures to Willie Lynch. Some argue that the white controlled system is responsible. To accept this, is to accept the belief that we are as inferior, as a race of people, as white social engineering would have us believe. Are we destined to always look to someone else for our salvation? We did that during and after the Katrina hurricane. Is it the fault of white folk that we fail to realize our full potential as a society, or is it time that we look to ourselves as the villain?

DESTINY IN OUR HANDS . . .
THE SEEDS OF A NEW SOCIETY

After the Civil War it became possible for Blacks to vote in the south, this was made possible as a result of the passage of the Reconstruction Acts by Congress. Five states had a majority Black population: Alabama, Florida, Louisiana, Mississippi, and South Carolina. Prior to the Reconstruction Acts, which were given more support by the Fourteenth and Fifteenth Amendments to the Constitution, there were 627,000 White voters in the south and no Black voters. After the Civil war Blacks gained the right to vote, and there were 703,000 who did so. Consequently, it became possible for Blacks to hold office on a local and statewide basis.

All of the early Black congressmen (and senators) were members of the Republican Party. This was because the Republicans, exemplified by President Abraham Lincoln, were the party in office during the Civil War and the party to which many abolitionists belonged.

The Democrats were opposed to all attempts to banish slavery. Thirteen of the twenty-two Blacks elected to Congress during Reconstruction were ex-slaves and all were self-taught or family trained. There were seven lawyers, three ministers, one banker, one publisher, two school teachers, and three college presidents. Eight had experience in state assemblies and senates. There were problems, however, as five of the first twenty Blacks elected to the House were denied their seats and ten others had their terms interrupted or delayed. Claims of vote fraud were the most common ploy used by Whites to deny an elected Black person his seat.

In 1869 James Lewis, John Willis Menard, and Pinckney B.S. Pinchback—all of Louisiana—were elected and never seated. In 1870 Joseph H. Rainey of South Carolina was the first Black to be seated in the House. He ran for reelection in 1872, won, and in 1874 his reelection was challenged. He was seated in the House, after several months, when the House member voted to seat him. He won again in 1876, and was again challenged. He was seated and after eighteen months the investigating committee recommended his seat be declared vacant. The full House, however, did not vote on the matter and referred it back to the committee.

Other Blacks who were elected to the House and seated often had very rocky tenures. Only a few did not have to face hostile, organized opposition within Congress. A few examples are listed below.

- Robert C. DeLarge, South Carolina, elected in 1870
  His election was challenged from the beginning and the challenge resulted in him serving twenty-two months out of twenty-four. The seat was declared vacant for the final two months.

- Josiah Thomas Walls, Florida, elected in 1870
  Wells was the only Black representative unseated twice by opponents challenging his elections.

- Jefferson Franklin Long, Georgia, elected in 1871
  Served an abbreviated term in 1871 (the election he won was held to fill an abbreviated term). White congressional opposition and intimidation of Black voters led to him not being reelected.

- Robert Brown Elliott, South Carolina, elected in 1871
  An attorney before he entered politics, Elliott served two consecutive terms. He was also able to read, German, Spanish, French, and Latin.

- Joseph H. Rainey, South Carolina, elected in 1871
  Served two consecutive terms, but as usual, the environment in Congress, especially from White southern representatives, was very hostile.

- Alonzo J. Ransier, Georgia, elected in 1872
  Succeeded Robert C. DeLarge. He was Lt. Governor before he
  won DeLarge's seat.

- James T. Rapier, Alabama, elected in 1873
  He served two consecutive terms and lost in 1875 when many
  ballot boxes were stolen and destroyed and replaced with others
  containing stuffed or illegally cast ballots. There was also armed
  intimidation of Black voters by Whites.

- John Mercer Langston, Virginia, elected in 1888
  The only Black person ever elected to Congress from Virginia,
  Mercer was denied his seat for almost two years.

- Thomas E. Miller, South Carolina, elected in 1889
  He served one term and afterwards was named president of the
  State Colored College at Orangeburg, South Carolina.

During Reconstruction, southern Whites suddenly found themselves
looking at former slaves not only eyeball to eyeball, but as equals before
the law and in their (the freed slaves) ability to obtain elected office.
Many Whites never ceased trying to "turn back the clock" so to speak.

In Reconstruction's place segregation was instituted and voting
rights for Blacks ceased. Thus, toward the end of the 19th century, it
became virtually impossible for Blacks in the south to be elected to
any office. This reality did not change until the mid-1960s.

THE NEW BEGINNING

*"Lincoln assigned Gen. O. O. Howard to head the bureau and
administer its tasks, which were: to make as rapidly as possible
a general survey of conditions and needs in every state and*

> *locality; to relieve immediate hunger ad distress; to appoint state*
> *commissioners and upwards of 900 bureau officials; to put the*
> *laborers to work at regular wage; to transport laborers, teachers,*
> *and officials; to furnish land for the peasant; to open schools;*
> *to pay bounties to Black soldiers and their families; to establish*
> *hospitals and guard health; to administer justice between man and*
> *former master; to answer continuous and persistent criticism, north*
> *and south, Black and white; to find funds to pay for all this."*

The abolitionist movements in the North including churches and philanthropic organizations "began the systematic teachings of Negroes and poor whites." They instituted day, night, and industrial schools, Sunday schools and colleges. They began the training of Black teachers. Most of the present Black colleges, like Howard (named after the general and bureau head), Fisk (named after Gen. Fisk), and Atlanta, were "founded or substantially aided in their earliest days by the Freedman's Bureau." The hospitals and medical care system made tremendous inroads into the Black death rate.

In addition to this, several banks had been established for Blacks: Gen. Banks established one in New Orleans in 1864; Gen. Butler and Gen. Saxton established several in South Carolina. As a result of these beginnings, Lincoln signed the law on March 3rd to incorporate the Freemen's Savings and Trust Company (Freedman's Bank). The thrift of the Blacks astonished the whites both north and south. The ex-slaves' bank had total deposits at one time of 57 million dollars. At first these savings were protected by provisions declaring that investments be made in government securities. But an amendment was passed in Congress in 1870, which allowed half the holdings invested in United States Bonds to be invested in other "notes and bonds secured by real estate mortgages." The Freedmen's savings were then loaned recklessly to speculators, ultimately leading to the bank's decline. (An effort was made to dump this mess on Douglass as a representative of the Black man.)

BLACK CODES

The end of the Reconstruction Era was successful through the imposition of "Black Codes," laws. These laws were designed to limit Black participation in all areas of life. These laws helped in the establishment of sanctioned violence and "control" on the local level by the Ku Klux Klan, the active and passive aid—via passing legislation and refusing to act when called upon in certain circumstances—of Presidents Andrew Johnson, Ulysses S. Grant, and Rutherford B. Hayes. Whites encouraged by President Johnson's evident intention to return to them the management of their own affairs, Southern legislators, elected by white voters, passed what came to be called Black Codes. Their very evident purpose was to reduce free blacks to a new kind of legal servitude distinguished by all the disadvantages of slavery and none of its advantages—a state, many argued, that was worse than slavery itself.

The Black Codes were not the result of a brief lapse in judgment on the part of Southern legislatures or the work of extremists, but rose, rather, out of the famous grassroots and indicated by an ordinance passed immediately after the war in the small town of Opelousas, Louisiana. The ordinance stated that "no negro or freedmen shall be allowed to come within the limits of the town of Opelousas without special permission from his employers . . . . Whoever shall violate this provision shall suffer imprisonment and two days work on the public streets, or pay a fine of five dollars." Any Negro found on the streets of the town after ten o'clock in the evening had to work for five days on the public streets or pay a $5 fine. The ordinance further provided:

"No Negro or freedman shall be permitted to rent or keep a house within the limits of the town under any circumstances . . . . No Negro or freedman shall reside within the limits of the town . . . who is not in the regular service of some white person or former owner . . . . No public meetings or congregations of Negroes or freedmen shall be allowed within the limits of the town . . . . No negro or freedman shall be permitted to preach, exhort, or otherwise declaim to congregations of colored people without a special permission from the mayor or president of the board of police . . . No freedman . . . shall be allowed to carry firearms, or any kind of weapons . . . . No freedman shall sell, barter, or exchange any article of merchandise within the limits of Opelousas without permission in writing from his employer." In the parish of St. Landry it was required "that every negro is to be in the service of some white person, or former owner.

The Black Codes were the diabolical beginning to the end of all the gains made by African Americans as a result of the Civil War. By the end of the war, blacks had established an educational system, banking system, healthcare system, and a political structure. These institutions are the foundation of any society, thus should have been the beginning of Black society. In 1870, something in our genes allowed all of this to be taken from black Americans. The results were what we are trying to overcome over 150 years later. The fact that we allowed ourselves to be re-enslaved is troubling. What in their character would allow the Black Codes to suck the life out of a newly freed people without a fight? You would have to wonder if they were depending on someone else other than themselves to protect their rights. Would it not have been better to die a free man than, rather than to live another 150 years as a slave? There was no one else to save us, but ourselves. We chose not to do so. We chose, as Willie Lynch said, "to trust and believe in whites, to protect us." So we trusted. Even to this day we still trust. Anyone promising civil rights to 20 million eligible voters can get their vote without question or performance. We should control our future through the political system. We can take our rights, just by voting. Why won't the so-called Black leadership tell us that? Instead, they say, "Vote Democrat."

2

MARRIAGE IS FOR WHITE PEOPLE

In an article that appeared in the Washington Post, an interesting insight was gained in the thought process of young African American males in relationship to their views of family responsibility. Portions of the article sighted below were troubling from the perspective of their concept of what they saw as their role as fathers in a family.

Though troubling relative to their view of their relationship to their parental partner, it is comforting to note that they were willing to step up to their role as fathers. Yet, they have no clue of how to be a "real man" and feel good about doing so; how to stand tall as a man without having a subservient female partner.

"Marriage Is for White People"

"That's what one of my students told me some years back during a career exploration class for sixth-graders at an elementary school in Southeast Washington, DC. I was pleasantly surprised when the boys in the class stated that being a good father was a very important goal to them, more meaningful than making money or having a fancy title."

"That's wonderful!" I told my class. "I think I'll invite some couples in to talk about being married and rearing children."

"Oh, no," objected one student. "We're not interested in the part about marriage, only about how to be good fathers."

And that's when the other boy chimed in, speaking as if the words left a nasty taste in his mouth: "Marriage is for white people."

"He's right, at least statistically. The marriage rate for African Americans has been dropping since the 1960s, and today, we have the lowest marriage rate of any racial group in the United States. In 2001, according to the U.S. Census, 43.3 percent of black men and 41.9 percent of black women in America had never been married, in contrast to 27.4 percent and 20.7 percent respectively for whites. African American women are the least likely in our society to marry. In the period between 1970 and 2001, the overall marriage rate in the United States declined by 17 percent; but for blacks, it fell by 34 percent. Such statistics have caused Howard University relationship therapist Audrey Chapman to point out that African Americans are the most uncoupled people in the country."

"How have we gotten here? What has shifted in African American customs, in our community, in our consciousness that has made marriage seem so unnecessary or unattainable?"

"Although slavery was an atrocious social system, men and women back then nonetheless often succeeded in establishing working families. In his account of slave life and culture, "Roll, Jordan, Roll," historian Eugene D. Genovese wrote: "A slave in Georgia prevailed on his master to sell him to Jamaica so that he could find his wife, despite warnings that his chances of finding her on so large an island were remote . . . . Another slave in Virginia chopped his left hand off with a hatchet to prevent being sold away from his son." I was stunned to learn that a black child was more likely to grow up living with both parents during slavery days than he or she is today, according to sociologist Andrew J. Cherlin. Traditional notions of family, especially the extended family network, endure. But working mothers, unmarried couples living together, out-of-wedlock births, birth control, divorce and remarriage have transformed the social landscape. And no one seems to feel this more than African American women. One told me that with today's changing morals, it's hard to know "what normal looks like" when it comes to courtship, marriage and parenthood. Sex, love and childbearing have become a la carte choices rather than a package deal that comes with marriage. Moreover, in an era of brothers on the "down low," the spread of sexually transmitted diseases and the decline of the stable blue-collar jobs that black men used to hold, linking one's fate to a man makes marriage a risky business for a black woman."

"A woman who takes that step is bold and brave," one young single mother told me. "Women don't want to marry because they don't want to lose their freedom."

The previous characterization of relationships between black males and females did not consider the history of black males in this country. To this day, we are a product of a diabolical strategy of social engineering to destroy any confidence of the black female in her man to protect and provide for her and her children. The strategy was simple, drive a wedge between the male and his family by dehumanizing, and minimizing him. Make the female believe that the white male master was the only one who could protect and provide for her. That is a strongly held perception to this day, 150 years later.

Those perceptions are constantly reinforced daily through the negative black male images in the media. You are more likely to see a Crack head black male in a televised news interview than an articulate black male. Black males are portrayed as fun loving, womanizing, and crack head thugs. The image that you are more likely to see is that he is usually uneducated and jobless, or that he is a bling-bling grilled up rapper that exploits young women. All of these images are designed to perpetuate the perception that black males are lazy, undependable, ignorant, and juvenile. As a result, we have developed a society where black men are viewed to have very little value, minimal education, minimal job experience, and a host of identity problems.

The present day black family's philosophy would be to place a higher priority on college educating the girls rather than the boys. Ill-prepared men can not provide for a family. So it is easier to not take on the responsibility of a family.

I would like to think that the response of the boys in the Washington Post article was more a reflection of frustration about their inability to function as parent and provider, in a family environment, than their unwillingness to do so. An examination of the possible solutions was recommended in an article by Ramesh Ponnuru and Richard Nadler for National Review, March 5, 2001.

"This problem has to be approached using a two-tiered process. First, we (the elders) have to realize that we do not prepare young people for taking leadership roles in our community. Why do we celebrate the blues but denigrate hip-hop? Why don't we distinguish between the major thinkers among our youth and the thugs? We bare the responsibility for the lost generations of our people. Even if we see their actions as self-defeating and self-hating, we have to take responsibility for having allowed this situation to occur.

On the other hand, why do we get so upset when young men and women also want to identify with their other racial/ethnic sides? Are we afraid that they're trying to abandon us? Do we want to hold them back so that they don't have a broader and more sophisticated view of their identities? Don't we know that this is their world and it is our job to support them while they gain a solid footing?

These are only the first few questions we should ask, and answer. And as we respond, we should edit out all cynicism and derogatory notions from our voices and words. These young people are our only hope. We have to liberate them where we can, decriminalize them when necessary, detoxify them if possible—but most importantly, we have to hear what they're telling us and make way for their leadership.

And to the youth I say, you have to take the reins. You have to realize that many members of the older generation have gotten what they wanted out of the Struggle. They aren't worried about the problems of America's urban youth, at least not enough to, once again, charge the ramparts and put what they have on the line. Revolutions (both violent and nonviolent) are manned by the young. Older people have retirement accounts and diseases to support, weak constitutions and a justified fear of imprisonment. We have fallen to the rear of the column. You, the urban youth of America, must begin to lead us.

If you, the youth, do not forgive us for fumbling, our race will be very far behind in the twenty-first century. And if we lose, the world suffers because most of America is on the wrong road already."

WELFARE—MAILBOX MONEY

The introduction of Welfare was another major contributor to the demise of the black family. It destroyed the will to work, to succeed, and the need for education. It reinforced, once again, the Willie Lynch philosophy of "IT IS NECESSARY THAT YOUR SLAVES TRUST AND DEPEND ON US. THEY MUST LOVE,

RESPECT AND TRUST ONLY US," thus the insidiousness of welfare.

Welfare was a tool, like the Black Code; use to maintain economic control over a sector of society, African Americans. The true purpose of welfare was not economic uplifting; the true purpose of welfare was to keep blacks from competing for the wealth of America. You did not have to be educated to go to the mail box. Ambition breeds competition, competition for white economic dominance. So, we took the check.

WELFARE DIED AUGUST 1996—RIP

Thanks to President Bill Clinton today welfare died.

"Throughout his campaign, Bill Clinton vowed to "end welfare as we know it." In an oft-repeated formulation, he promised to "provide people with the education, training, job placement assistance, and child care they need for two years—so that they can break the cycle of dependency. After two years, those who can work will be required to go to work, either in the private sector or in meaningful community-service jobs."

"As proposed thus far, Clinton's plan would take the essential elements of the Family Support Act and give them a stronger bite. The Act does not force participants to work, simply requiring what is often a short stint in job training or other activities. Clinton, on the other hand, wanted recipients to receive a full two years of training and education, which could include college classes. At the end of these two years, The Clinton plan required recipients to work or leave welfare, whereas before, they would have received benefits indefinitely.

The Clinton success refocused the national attention on the problem of long-term welfare dependency.

Improving the skills of welfare mothers is essential. Without more to offer employers, many mothers will never be able to earn enough to support themselves and their families. This is a major reason why they are on welfare in the first place.

The Clinton plan promised to give welfare recipients up to two years of education, job training, job placement assistance, child care, and additional health coverage. Advocates of the two-year time limit say it is just a convenient measure of dependency. Many recipients go off after much shorter periods.

Welfare dependency is, to a large extent, due to a lack of skills and training of unwed mothers, who form the bulk of long-term welfare recipients. Years of inactivity leave their mark. These young mothers, who start with poor prospects, further limit their life chances by dropping out of school, by having babies out of wedlock, and by not working. As a result, they do not have the education, skills, or work habits needed to earn a satisfactory living.

For many young mothers, training—at least as we know it—is too little, too late. Even richly-funded demonstration programs find it exceedingly difficult to improve the ability of these women to care for their children, let alone to become economically self-sufficient. It should be noted that most programs don't even try to work with fathers."

The cornerstone of every society is the family, from which flow all ambitions and dreams, human values, nurturing, loving and caring. Historically, the black family was headed by a matriarch. Historically black women were the strong, focused, loving, symbols of the black family.

As a direct result of social engineering the black male became mostly impudent, this invariably made the black female the center of strength in black community. The black family was functional until the 1960s, when a strange phenomenon overwhelmed it, "WHITE WOMEN'S LIBERATION." Black women wanted to be like white women, liberated. Black women could never be like white women, because they had already achieved what white women were trying to attain—respect and dominance in family affairs. To become liberated like white women, black women had to forsake their role as the family matriarch. When she chose this direction, she left the family without direction, value, and purpose. She became centered on self. This also gave the frustrated, directionless black male a reason to opt out. He became a major player in the further destruction of the family. Black males became assertive in the wrong direction. They tried to find dignity and self respect in all the wrong ways. The result was that they became self destructive.

The children were ultimately the victims, having to be raised in fatherless homes. As a male single parent of three children, I am the first to say, though not impossible, it is extremely difficult to be successful at raising a child as a single parent. The growing up process for children requires the contribution of both parents. Plants can only grow successfully with both sunlight and water. Children grow successfully with both parents. Something has crept into black society's mindset that considers the family unit as incontinent.

In the new family order, there are no matriarchs, no value center, and no direction. In the new family, granny is sometimes twenty six years older than her granddaughter. There is no granddad, just Tyrone. The end result is the new attitude which is reflective of an article that appeared in the Washington Post: "*Marriage is for White People*".

Ten years after Bill Clinton capitulated to Republican demands and signed on to watershed welfare-reform legislation, policy wonks, pro-family activists and politicians waging war on the welfare state have reason to celebrate as millions of former welfare recipients have joined the workforce.

ASSISTED GENOCIDE

There is one consistent thread that runs through this saga of racism—the control of wealth. The Civil Rights Act of the 1960's, like the Emancipation Proclamation of the 1860's created a competition for the control of wealth in this country. It gave legal power to large numbers of black people to compete for jobs and to build wealth. Once again, to some white people, black people became a serious threat in the competition for wealth. Thus in the late 1960s came the introduction of drugs in the black community. Drugs had the same insidious effect as welfare and the Black Codes—it destroyed the will to prosper.

Drugs destroyed the fabric of the new economic force in this country during the 1960s. To control a community's addiction is to build a dependency as stated by Willie Lynch, "*IT IS NECESSARY THAT YOUR SLAVES TRUST AND DEPEND ON US. THEY MUST LOVE, RESPECT AND TRUST ONLY US.*"

Prior to the 1960s, some black people were mostly functioning alcoholics; after the 1960s we became an addicted society. There was some drug use in the black community, but when it became apparent that something had to be done to control the black problem, somewhere in the bowels of white society it was decided that drugs were the solution.

Later there were investigations into allegations that the CIA was directly involved in the importation of large quantities of drugs into the country, subsequently in the black communities. It was also speculated that the CIA was directly involved in setting up distribution networks in all the major black communities across the country. This was never proven, though it was obvious that blacks were not capable of such an undertaken.

The introduction of drugs had a devastating effect on the once again freed black slaves, an effect that haunts us to this day, 50 years later. Welfare and drugs destroyed the hopes and dreams of 36,000,000 people, and we were willing, active participants in that destruction. We should have exercised our rights to decide for our families and communities how we were going to live. Where was our moral center? We allowed drugs to almost destroy our communities, culture, and families.

One thing is very clear, the black community never had the capacity or resources to import or distribute drugs at the level necessary to take control of its community. I waited everyday to hear someone say, "You are participating in your own destruction, stop it." Efforts to take control of this problem did not start until it became a white problem as well—especially within the white suburbs.

Today there is a new deep dark secret in this country called Methamphetamine. With the introduction of poly drugs (methamphetamine) the new epidemic has infected white, Middle America more than the black community. Black folk don't do poly drugs. Since poly drugs don't have to be imported; it's cooked in the bathtub, it poses a particularly difficult challenge for law enforcement structure. I suspect that drug use has gone down in the black community and is at an epidemic level in white, Middle America. (Can't prove it, just suspect it). This is not something that would be widely reported in the media. There is one fact that studies have verified; the reported rate of addiction in the black community is far lower than is consistently reported. Why is this important, because the drug use image has been used to define us as a race?

IT TAKES A VILLAGE

Over the past forty years black families have had to endure a planned assault on the cornerstone of any society, the family.

Prior to the beginning of the civil rights movement of the early sixties, black families remained a traditional social unit, with a father, mother, and children. There was also a supportive extended family structure. The stability of this structure created a challenge to whites with limited education and vocational training because it created competition in the job market for the same jobs.

The de-education of blacks was achieved through the integration of schools in non-integrated neighborhoods. Whites moved to reestablish segregated schools that were sufficiently funded school systems in segregated neighborhoods with strong tax bases, leaving black schools in poor neighborhoods with low, insufficient tax bases. Thus, began the creation of a really bad education for black kids with the intent of killing their ability to be competitive in the economic market place. African Americans are now in the process of rebuilding the foundation of any society, the family unit and a productive educational system.

REESTABLISHING FATHERHOOD

In nineteen sixty only nine percent of all children lived in single-parent homes. Presently in the United States, almost one third of children are born to single mothers. A larger number of children will see their parents divorced before their eighteenth birthday. Two third of black kids are born out of wedlock. Over half of American children will spend all or part of their childhood without their father in the home.

Robert Rector of the Heritage Foundation cited that the collapse of marriage is the principal cause of child poverty and other social problems. Half of the children are living without the support and attention of their fathers, and have never been in their father's home, or those over the age of four never saw their fathers at least once a week. Those statistics must change.

Though the effort should be applauded, It is too much to expect a single mother to raise a boy to become a man. In most societies it is the responsibility of the elder men to assist in the development of boys into men. It now must be the responsibility of the elder or mature African American males to prepare the young men.

The time is now for the black college fraternities and sororities to share in the mentoring and surrogate fathering of young fatherless black kids. It is not too much to ask fraternities and sororities to take on the responsibility for mentoring those fatherless kids by sponsoring a monthly breakfast to just talk.

New elders, it is time to step up. It's your turn. It takes a village . . . There should be a similar expectation of the sororities. Reach back, take a struggling little girl by the hand, and show her the way. Success would only require an honest commitment, because contrary to popular belief, black kids have very high self-esteem.

Although it is a common myth that black youth are likely to have low self-esteem, studies in the last few decades have shown them to feel just as good, if not better, about themselves and as self-confident, in general, as white youth; the only thing that they need are direction and guidance. They need someone to teach them life skills, someone to show them the way. Step up Greek sisters and brothers.

3

EDUCATIONAL CHOICE
SCHOOLS OF DREAMS

"There is a brilliant child locked inside every student . . ."

During a recent visit to a friend's home, I had an opportunity to observe a one year old kid named Josiah with an interesting problem. He was in the kitchen with his parents riding his scooter. After a while he decided to ride in the hallway; however he had a problem, he could not get his scooter over lip of the doorway into the hall. He first tried to ride over the obstruction without success. He than backed up, got a running start—no success.

After several attempts he stopped and just sat there on his scooter. My first instinct was to help him, but I hesitated for a moment instead. As I moved to help him, he got off the scooter, pulled it up to the obstruction, proceeded to lift the front wheel over the obstruction, walked to the rear where he proceeded to push the scooter's rear wheels to the obstruction. Josiah lifted the rear wheels over the obstruction, mounted his scooter, and proceeded happily down the hallway.

I mention this incident because a number of things happened that dispels the myth that black kids are intellectually inferior. I don't think that Josiah is special. I just think that his parents do not limit his expectations. In that situation Josiah, a one year old, faced a problem; came up with a solution; solved the problem; and continue on his merry way.

The only limits on black kids are those imposed by a sometimes racist society, or their parents. Josiah is now five years old with an insatiable curiosity and the ability to satisfy it. Let him go . . . let him grow. To do that, the educational system for black kids must be reformed.

Hungry at School and at Home

Teachers in at-risk communities report that Mondays and Fridays are the hardest days for discipline. On Mondays, many children return to school from a tough weekend, some having not eaten much, and can act out or be unfocused. And for kids whose greatest stability occurs at school, Friday is a reminder of what they're going back into.

Teachers have begun to notice more kids coming to school with headaches, stomach aches and dizziness. Many of these kids had trouble paying attention in class, created disruptions, or lacked overall motivation. These issues, it was discovered, had a common source: hunger. Before long, a solution was developed: Provide students with take home food packs, in addition to the School Lunch Program.

SCHOOL CHOICE

In most public school systems children are assigned to a school according to their home address. People with financial resources have school choice, because they can afford to either move to an area with better schools or send their children to a private school. Parents without such means are stuck with the school assigned to them, regardless of its quality or fit to that child. Today, there are options, such as federally funded and mandated school choice.

I am always amazed at how easy it is to excuse, or explain away, why black kids can't read, when in reality, in my opinion, there are three environmental conditions that, obviously, must exist if learning in the classroom is to be effective:

1. Safety—Kids must feel safe in their learning environment; they learn better in a non-conflict environment.

2. Expectation—If you don't expect anything, you won't get anything. Children must be challenged.

3. Structure—To be successful, children must have programs that fit their learning interest, learning capacity, and realistic future expectations.

School choice refers to the practice of offering parents and students a variety of educational opportunities. Common choice options include magnet programs within the public school system, charter schools, and voucher programs. In the 1980s and 1990s, the "school choice movement" garnered significant attention from parents, educators, and policymakers seeking new methods of reforming public education. Public education reform is currently a foremost issue at the local, state, and national level.

Full school choice programs, also known as tuition vouchers programs, provide parents with a portion of the public educational funding allotted for their child to attend public school, or allow them to use these funds to attend the school of their choice. Such a school might be a private school, a religious or parochial school, or a neighborhood or magnet public school.

Private scholarship programs and charter schools are two other forms of school choice. Charter schools provide an alternative to the cookie-cutter city/state district school model.

School voucher programs are not new. Since 1869, the state of Vermont has had a law authorizing "tuitioning" in which the state pays for children to attend private schools in towns without public institutions.

Voucher Programs

Voucher programs award students all or part of their allocated public education funds to apply toward tuition at a private or public school of their choice. The label "voucher program" is encompassing. Included in the label are publicly and privately funded programs and, occasionally, tax-assistance or tax-credit options. Overall, students using voucher programs account for less than 1 percent of the national school-age population.

Whether voucher programs are successful in raising student achievement is a point of sometimes contentious debate and frequently depends upon the rigor of the study itself. Recent evaluations of voucher programs, including the Manhattan Institute's study of the Children's Scholarship Fund in Charlotte as well as studies of the New York, Dayton, and Washington D.C. privately-funded voucher programs, suggest that there are statistically significant achievement gains for low-income students, particularly African-American students, attending private schools through vouchers and scholarships. In Charlotte, for example, improvement gains after one year in attendance were between 5.4 and 7.7 percentile points for math and reading standardized scores.[2]

In Chicago, Marva Collins, an African American educator, created a low cost private school specifically for the purpose of teaching low income African American children whom the public school system had labeled as being "learning disabled." One article about Marva Collins' school stated, "Working with students having the worst of backgrounds, those who were working far below grade level, and even those who had been labeled as 'unteachable,' Marva was able to overcome the obstacles.

News of third grade students reading at ninth grade level, four-year-olds learning to read in only a few months, outstanding test scores, disappearance of behavioral problems, second-graders studying Shakespeare, and other incredible reports, astounded the public."[3]

During the 2006-2007 school year, Collins' school charged $5,500 for tuition, and parents said that the school did a much better job than the Chicago public school system. Meanwhile, during the 2007-2008 year, Chicago public school officials claimed that their budget of $11,300 per student was not enough.[4]

There is a destructive determination by some sectors of society to force a failing policy on every child in the Public School system. In most instances, kids aren't motivated to learn, they are forced to learn.

The Harlem Children Zone

The Harlem Children's Zone is a program that was profiled in a book by Paul Tough, Whatever It Takes.[5]

The Zone is the brainchild of Geoffrey Canada, an African American man in his mid-50s who grew up in extreme poverty in the South Bronx. Canada escaped the inner city for Bowdoin and Harvard and then returned to New York to try to create better options for kids like the ones he grew up with.

In the mid-'90s, he was running a decent-size nonprofit for teenagers in Harlem, where everyone told him how successful he was. But he could see only the kids he wasn't helping. Poor children in Harlem faced so many disadvantages, he realized, that it didn't make sense to address just one or two and ignore the rest. A great after-school program wouldn't do much good if the school itself were lousy. And even the best school would have a hard time succeeding without help from the parents.

Canada's solution was to take on all those problems simultaneously. The Harlem Children's Zone takes a holistic approach, following children from cradle to college, mimicking the cocoon of stimulation and support that surrounds middle-class children.

The Zone now enrolls more than 8,000 children a year in its various programs, which cover a 97-block section of central Harlem. "We're not interested in saving 100 kids," Canada told me once. "Even 300 kids, even 1,000 kids to me is not going to do it. We want to be able to talk about how you save kids by the tens of thousands, because that's how we're losing them. We're losing kids by the tens of thousands."[5]

Canada believes that many poor parents aren't doing enough to prepare their kids for school—not because they don't care, but because they simply don't know the importance of early childhood stimulation. So the Zone starts with Baby College, nine weeks of parenting classes that focus on discipline and brain development. It continues with language-intensive prekindergarten, which feeds into a rigorous K-12 charter school with an extended day and an extended year. That academic "conveyor belt," as Canada calls it, is supplemented by social programs: family counseling, a free health clinic, after-school tutoring, and a drop-in arts center for teenagers.

Canada's early childhood programs are in many ways a response to research showing that the vocabularies of poor children usually lag significantly behind those of middle-class children. At the Harlem Gems prekindergarten, four-year-olds were bombarded with books, stories, and flash cards—including some in French. The parents were enlisted, too; one morning, frequently families are taken on a field trip to a local supermarket organized by the Harlem Children's Zone. The point wasn't to learn about nutrition, but rather about language—how to fill an everyday shopping trip with the kind of nonstop chatter that has become second nature to most upper-middle-class parents, full of questions about numbers and colors and letters and names. That chatter, social scientists have shown, has a huge effect on vocabulary and reading ability.[6] And as we walked through the aisles, those conversations were going on everywhere: Is the carrot bumpy or smooth? What color is that apple? How many should we buy?

So far, Canada's vision has yielded impressive results. Last year, the first conveyor-belt students reached the third grade and took their first statewide standardized tests. In reading, they scored above the New York City average, and in math they scored well above the state average.[7]

Obama's proposal is to replicate the Harlem Children's Zone in 20 cities across the country. In his speech announcing the plan, he proposed that each new zone operate as a 50-50 partnership between the federal government and local philanthropists, businesses, and governments, and he estimated that the federal share of the cost would come to "a few billion dollars a year." It's an undertaking that would mark a seismic change in the way that we approach poverty.[8]

In Washington, D.C., until the 1970s, the Public school system used the Track System of course selection. It was structured to allow students to choose between the College Prep., General Studies, and Industrial Arts. These three program tracks allowed students to choose, based on their interest, future goals expectations, and learning prep. This system recognized that everyone had different learning interests and abilities; therefore by structuring programs that catered to those differences, kids look forward to that time of the day when their chosen courses were offered. The results were that kids were excited about learning.

Students in the College Prep. Track (Advance Placement) were offered challenging classes designed to prepare that student for college.

The student in the General Studies track were taught labor marketable skills, i.e., clerical skills that were tailored for the local labor market (Local and Federal governments). Very few kids graduated without having skills necessary for entry level positions in the local job market.

The Industrial Arts students learned trades and craft skills that allowed them to go immediately into the jobs market upon graduating. These skills included Brick mason, Carpentry, Sheet metal, Auto mechanics, electrical repair and plumbing. With this preparation, they would be eligible to apply for union training programs. Those kids became the nucleus of the local black middle class of today. In most educational systems today, these options do not exist.

Today, in most educational systems (including the DC system), the above options rarely exist. In the current educational systems, black male students are failures by any standard, at an alarming rate. Currently only 25% of all graduating classes are black males. There seem to be little effort to develop and institute creative solutions to correct the problem. One possible solution might be Single Sex education.

ADOLESCENSE—THE CRAZY YEARS

Youthful mid-life crisis

It must be noted that I have no academic credentials to support the following views that I will offer. My views are those of a black male single parent of two boys and two girls.

THE SAME SEX EDUCATION OPTION

The Harlem Children's Zone primarily focuses on the early developing years of a child. Though critical in the development of young minds, we must not loose site of the equally critical stage of the middle years, the adolescent years, the crazy years. The adolescent years are the years of major distractions ie., identity crisis, and hormonal upheavals. It appears to have a more profound effect on the boys than girls, though the young female body is biologically changing also. The following are suggested as voluntary options within the school district for parents of kids during the crazy years.

There has been research documenting the performance of a Florida school that has separated some of its pupils.8 Kathy Piechura-Couture, Stetson University education professor said her research shows that separating boys and girls can be beneficial, although it's not a magic bullet.[9]

Her research found that the third year of a recent program, boys who attend class together tend to outperform boys in mixed classes in reading and math to a degree that is statistically significant. [10]

Girls also tend to do better, although the results aren't as consistent.[11]

Although the research is mixed, some studies suggest low-income children in urban schools learn better when separated from the opposite sex.[12] The concern about boys' performance in a secondary educational environment has also driven some of the interest in same-sex education. Socially, same-sex schools are emotionally easier on students. Stereotypes based on gender are not a huge issue in these settings. Girls are more outspoken and competitive when boys are not around to tease them. They also feel more comfortable participating in sports and other traditionally male dominated fields. [13]

Program like these should be strictly voluntary. They should start in the forth grade and end in the tenth grade. The suggested starting grade gives a child the opportunity to become socially acclimated prior to reinforcing academic discipline. The ending grade also gives a socially insecure adolescent an opportunity to gain social self confidence. [14]

The same sex environment offers the ideal opportunity for male/female mentoring. I have always been an advocate of adults participating in small group meals. Breakfast gives an adult the perfect opportunity to have open discussions on current events, social issues, and sometimes even personal problems. In most black families, this activity would never take place, because most black families don't have the luxury of time for this type activity due to work schedules. The mentoring aspect is so very important to adolescent kids, who in most instances grow up in single parent homes.

In 1990, only 9 percent of all children lived in single-parent households.[1] Presently in the United States, almost one third of children are born to single mothers.[16] A larger number of children

---

[1]   Excerpts from Ordinary Children, Extraordinary Teachers and Marva Collins' Way.

will see their before parents divorced their eighteenth birthday. [17] Two third of black children are born out of wedlock.[18] Over half of American children will spend all or part of their childhood without their father in the home.[19] Same sex schools offer a unique opportunity for gender mentoring. These numbers indicate a pressing need for a race wide, structured mentoring program.

The continued effort of mixed gender based education has not been successful for sectors of the young black male population—so why not try a voluntary based same sex program in select school systems?

"The definition of insanity is doing the same over and over while expecting a different results,"[20]

SINGLE SEX EDUCATION

There is a natural bonding that takes place in a same sex environment, one that does not take place in a testosterone driven environment. There is a sense of fraternity and sisterhood that tend to build confidence, security, and caring that is present among the individual sexes, that is generally not possible in today's learning environment. I am not advocating that all schools should become single sex institutions, just that it should be one of the options available.

In explaining why African-American boys lag behind in school and deciding what to do about it. The following is a study conducted by Larry Davis, in 2003.

While recent stories in the national media on the academic achievement gap between boys and girls are important, the reporting in them contains new revelations for African-American parents or for officials at high schools and colleges that have even the smallest impact on the numbers of black students. They have been observing this gap among black boys and girls for years, and know, therefore, that it is far more dramatic among blacks than it is among the white students featured in most of the recent spate of media coverage. Every three bachelor's degrees awarded to blacks go to women, while women receive 56 percent of bachelor's degrees awarded to whites.

What causes this greater gender disparity among black youth; what are its implications and what can be done about it?

A research team embarked on a five-year study of a nationally representative inner-city, predominantly black high school. They managed to track 86 percent of entering freshmen over a four-year period and determined whether they stayed at the original school, transferred to another one, dropped out, landed in jail, left town or were killed. Only 60 percent of the entering class of black students graduated in four years, 71 percent of the females and only 46 percent of the males.

Contrary to popular belief, these youth had very high self-esteem. Although it is a common myth that black youth are likely to have low self-esteem, studies in the last few decades have shown them to feel just as good, if not better, about themselves and as self-confident, in general, as white youth.

However, what they did find was that black boys, relative to black girls, thought of themselves less capable academically and didn't feel confident about their ability to read and write and do schoolwork. They scored lower on academic self-efficacy—what might be called academic self-esteem.

By contrast, the girls had more favorable attitudes toward the academic process. They also felt they had more social support—that people around them thought it was important that they graduate and expected them to graduate.

With a large percentage of African-American males not graduating from high school, their job prospects in an era of vanishing blue-collar jobs are dismal. With the movement to get women graduate degrees, into work and moving up the career ladder, black women are advancing at an unprecedented rate while black males are dropping out. Where are the eligible, educated black men these women will marry and establish families with?

It has long been realized that it's a grave societal problem to have so many fewer black males educated than women.

As parents, policymakers, and educators search for solutions to the crisis in the nation's public schools, single sex education emerges time and again as a promising strategy, particularly for African American students. As the abstract indicates, the Bush Administration has indicated its support for sex separation and announced its intention to loosen the applicable legal standards to enable school districts to experiment with single sex schools and classes. This paper argues that, in order to comprehend fully the implications of single sex schooling in inner city schools, examining the history of sex-based and race-based segregation in education is essential.

On average, 60 percent of black male students in the United States do not graduate from high school.

When it comes to black males more receive a GED in prison than those that graduate from college.

BEHAVIOR AND BOREDOM

Many researchers today agree on several culprits at the root of this problem. For starters, the black male's social scene is fraught with traps that Vernon C. Polite, dean of the College of Education at

Eastern Michigan University, can rattle off: single-parent mothers too busy making a living to participate in the PTA and peer pressure that fires up boys' testosterone which sometimes results in violence, incorrigible behavior, acting out, chronic truancy—all problems that force a school to impose discipline standards at the cost of academics.

Even as early as grade school, it has been documented in far too many cases of how black boys' refusal to do schoolwork or pay attention in class has relegated them to special education classes reserved for the mentally and emotionally disturbed. Rosa A. Smith points to one young man she met while she was superintendent in Beloit, Wisc., whose chatter revealed a brilliant mind, yet his mother had to enroll him in a new school to prevent administrators at the previous elementary school from placing him in special education based on nothing more than his high-octane, easily bored personality.

Secondly, as most people on the front lines battling the achievement gap insist, schools aren't handing students a curriculum with bite. Smith says every school's mission should be to ensure its students are reading at or above grade level by grade three. "I tell people, forget the self-esteem classes. Teach them to read, and then to learn to love to read, and it will take care of so many self-esteem problems," she notes.

Many would contest that Polite's solution to both issues sounds elementary—especially the means to create an environment that centers on care and determining the need of the individual.

But even Polite admits the remedy requires a commitment of personal capital, involvement and understanding. Here's a look at the sweat equity and innovative thinking that went into changing these black boys' experiences.

In 2005, Louisa May Alcott students scored in the 93rd percentile on fourth-grade reading achievement, won one of three national

McGraw Hill Pride of SRA awards, an NCLB Blue Ribbon School of Excellence designation and an Ohio state award, The School of Promise.

The same mindset works at KIPP DC: KEY Academy as well. This public charter middle school in Washington, D.C., accepts open enrollment, so most fifth graders arrive two years behind grade level, scoring between 30 percent and 40 percent on tests. Here black males and others attend mandatory Saturday school, sit through longer class days, and wear uniform T-shirts that say "No short cuts, no excuses." In 2004-2005, the fifth graders shot to the 90th percentile in math.

"Its crazy growth, and it's because it is a very intense culture focused on math, reading, science and social studies," says KEY Academy Executive Director Susan Schaeffler.

Carlton P. Jordan, a researcher, applauds such efforts and urges educators to demand still more from black boys by infusing the curriculum with "intellectual stretch." "We can do standards . . . to make sure we're hitting the assessments," he explains. "But it's really how we think about those concepts—taking an historical read of a text, a Marxist read of a text, giving kids different ways to break it down and ask questions." Unfortunately, these kinds of questions are rarely posed outside an Advanced Placement class.

The brainstorming resulted in an experimental strategy dubbed M2EN (Minority Men Exceeding the Norms) rolled out in January where roughly 50 boys—identified as leaders among their peers, even if that power had been used in negative ways, as founder Dennis Lacewell, the social studies department chair, puts it—were assigned to groups called houses, such as of a fraternity structure, to win points for their group through academic, leadership, service and behavior goals. Failure subtracts points so the competition is co-relational. "It's

Harry Potter in the hood," Horan quips. "The main responsibilities are to support, uplift and challenge within a house, using the natural competition already present in the adolescent heart."

So the male teachers, known as elders, meet with their houses at 6:30 a.m., checking homework, tracking members' grades, and tackling additional reading and discussions. The group also took it upon themselves to raise grant money to fund field trips to Morehouse College in Atlanta, and bought prizes such as computer systems or cash to reward boys who made honor roll. Still, Horan counts the cost in human resources more so than dollars.

So far, North Lawndale has registered higher grade-point averages, better attendance, fewer disciplinary problems and an increased interest in leadership within the school among black male students. "Stop one of the kids in the hall and ask them to recite the poem Invictus. They can do it," he brags. "It appeals to the formational side as well as study skills, which make a lot of difference."

"We try to go overboard setting the examples for the young men, holding them accountable because they are bombarded by these negative images of minority men—on TV, when they walk through the neighborhood," says John Henry, a black history teacher. "We try to be in their face saying, 'Hey you can do these positive things. Look at us.'"

Yet Swanson, too, made an impact on this population even from her well-coiffed, blonde female vantage point. She drove into neighborhoods most whites labeled dangerous to talk with mothers and sons who had no idea who their father was. "I didn't understand everything about their community, but I needed to show I cared and I was there for them," she says. "Compassion doesn't mean, 'Oh I feel so sorry for you.' It's 'I will work with you and we will solve this.'"

To that end, she encourages teachers to demonstrate caring by showing interest in the black male's world-attend their sporting events and don't belittle boys' dreams of becoming the next Michael Jordan. She brought her young son to class to interact with her students. She even gave a stamp of approval to Ebonics—the controversial language among African-Americans that accepts sentences like "He be going"—as long as the students understood that grammatical English is the language of the professional world and could produce it when appropriate.

"My African-American males have always been just as successful as anybody else. Once they knew I wanted the best for them, there was no reason to resist me. A personal relationship and trust are huge," Swanson says.

"But don't confuse minority boys with vending machines," Polite cautions. Knowledge does not necessarily change a person's disposition, so knowing more about the home conditions and problems a student faces doesn't mean that a boy will magically change his attitude. "By that same token, it doesn't mean because they have a certain disposition they can't learn," he says.

"This is like an automobile factory. You can't refuse to work on the line because you don't like the model coming down the belt. Teachers have to work with the students they're given each year and find the keys that will make these kids the best they can be."

BOYS ONLY SCHOOL?

With these reasons, Smith has developed a supporting attitude toward same-sex schools. After all, the public Eagle Academy for Young Men in New York City took in anyone who applied for the first year in 2004-2005. Here boys and administrators breakfast together with conversations revolving around USA Today and New York Times articles on the table. A one-on-one mentoring program ensures that "if a boy is suspended here, you know a lot of people tried to work with him first," Smith points out.

As for accusations that this revives the ghosts of segregation, she's not buying. "Prince Charles didn't go to a co-ed school! To prepare to be king, he learned his lessons with other young men," she argues. "People with financial resources make this choice every day and we don't question it." Certainly it's accepted in the Bronx, where roughly 2,000 minority parents applied to enroll their boys in this environment in only its second year of existence.

"Far too many [Black and Hispanic] young men are not making it. Single-sex education may not be the answer but it is worth the try." David Banks, the principal at Eagle Academy, told a newspaper reporter. The only downside he's discovered so far: "Without the presence of young ladies to impress, the young men revert back to their natural playfulness." There's a good chance down the road Eagle Academy could find itself in the spotlight as the Schott Achievement Award winner for significant graduation rates among black boys—Smith's latest pilot. She's currently working with the Ohio State Department of Education to select three schools there that model good practices. "When you talk statistics, some people become overwhelmed. It's too big. We're going to show people it's possible and celebrate success and effort at the school level," she assures. "That's small enough for people to get their hands around."

Julie Sturgeon is a contributing editor.

EDUCATIONAL COMPETITON
CHARTER SCHOOLS

Freedom of choice: parents frustrated with conventional public schools are bucking the system. Here, black mothers who chose education alternatives share their success stories—Living Well Parenting Special. If an automaker produces lemons, drivers can steer their business elsewhere. Not so for parents depending on America's 94,000 public schools: When failing systems and antiquated curricula roll off the educational assembly line, our kids can't demand a recall.

Fortunately, there's a new model in development. It's called school choice, and the nation's 8 million Black students stand to benefit most. With school choice, parents can bypass troubled neighborhood schools and explore alternative routes, sending their kids to magnet programs, single-sex academies or independently run charter schools; using tuition vouchers for private or religious schools; or educating children at home.

The concept is compelling, if controversial. A persistent achievement gap between Black and White students-higher dropout rates, poorer reading skills—has rallied an unusual coalition of school-choice supporters, including Black educators and parents as well as conservative policy makers. Teachers' unions and other groups, however, contend that draining money and motivated students from struggling schools will only destroy public education. Still, alternative education is catching on. More than 40 percent of the nation's school districts today offer some form of choice.

These are the stories of five moms who've had success with school choice to share their stories, plus we tell you what you need to know to make the move.

SINGLE-SEX PUBLIC SCHOOLS

SUCCESS STORY: Donna Peart, 42, mother of Lauren, 13; The Bronx, New York

DILEMMA: Donna Peart attended an all-girls Catholic high school back in her native Jamaica. But there was no way she could afford the same thing for her daughter, Lauren—not in New York City on her temporary administrative assistant's salary and her husband's sales commissions. After much searching, Donna found a scholarship program called A Better Chance that sends bright low-income children of color to private college-prep schools. She applied, and Lauren, a math whiz, was among the lucky students accepted into the program.

But the middle school Lauren had her heart set on had no vacancies, and she was wait-listed. A Massachusetts boarding school offered a spot, but Donna and her husband weren't ready to send their 11-year-old that far from home. The local public middle school, where fights broke out daily, wasn't even an option.

SOLUTION: A counselor at the school that had wait-listed Lauren pointed Donna toward the Young Women's Leadership School of East Harlem. It was a 45-minute bus ride from the Pearts' house in The Bronx. Still, Donna thought she should at least take a look.

The school, founded by Ann Tisch, a former NBC reporter and the wife of media mogul Andrew Tisch, is one of only 18 single-sex public schools nationwide-and eight of those began operation within the past year. Research suggests that girls blossom academically in single-sex settings, partly because they aren't distracted by boys. Single-sex classes can also accommodate the different learning styles and brain development of boys and girls.

One visit to the school persuaded Donna. She noticed how poised the students seemed as they poured out the door. "Just like young ladies," Donna recalls. "Then I went upstairs and fell in love," she says: In the sun-filled classrooms, girls relaxed on sofas and chairs, reading and collaborating on projects. She saw "vibrant young teachers" take an interest in their students. The principal called them "my girls."

Donna was sold. Lauren wasn't thrilled. "All girls?!" she exclaimed. "That's boring!" But she took placement exams and was accepted. Now, after two years at Young Women's, she finds it anything but dull.

WHY IT WORKS FOR HER: Donna appreciates how the school has broadened Lauren's horizons. Lauren and her eighth-grade class have done health-science research at the New York Academy of Medicine and attended women-in-medicine classes at Stony Brook University's Manhattan campus. They've taken dance classes with the New York City Ballet and entertained such celebrity visitors as Oprah Winfrey and Senator Hillary Clinton. "The sky's the limit for them," marvels Donna. "They've developed a real sisterhood."

The school's rigorous curriculum (which requires Advanced Placement courses) and intensive college counseling (which starts in seventh grade; its college admissions rate has been 100 percent for the past three years) have put Lauren's dream of becoming an accountant within reach. "When you're in a coed school, the teachers pay more attention to the boys," Lauren says. "At this school I feel confident."

Fast Facts: The No Child Left Behind Act

* Gives students in low-performing schools the right to transfer to better ones or to receive tutoring and other supplemental services at local school district expense.

★ Requires school districts to annually test all children in grades three through eight in reading and math beginning in 2005, and to break down scores by race, income and ethnicity.

★ Includes funds that charter schools can use to purchase or renovate facilities. Also allows faith-based organizations to apply for federal grants to run after-school programs.

In the United States, a charter school is a school that is created via a legal charter. Usually (a) they are created with an express purpose or philosophy and (b) typically they are controlled in-house and not controlled by the local school district. Laws governing them vary from state to state.

Charter schools are an American school idea that allows publicly funded schools to act and operate like private schools. The theory is that competition from charter schools will force the other public schools to perform better.

Charter schools are commonly founded as magnet schools or as schools for at-risk kids or those with special educational needs.

Critics of charter schools as magnets claim they siphon off the best students and leave the public schools worse off. The National Education Association, the largest union of teachers, supports charter schools, so long as they have "the same standards of accountability and access as other public schools."

Opinions vary as to the success of charter schools, in part because of the philosophical outlook taken, and in part because—as may be expected—such schools vary one from another in quality, competence and effectiveness.

The first charter school opened in Minnesota in 1991, and as of the 2004-2005 school year, approximately 3,300 charter schools are in operation in 40 states and the District of Columbia, enrolling nearly 1 million students (National Charter School Directory, The Center for Education Reform Charter schools) reflect their founders' varied philosophies, programs, and organizational structures, serve diverse student populations, and are committed to improving public education.

Charter schools are freed of many restrictive rules and regulations. In return, these schools are expected to achieve educational outcomes within a certain period (usually three to five years) or have their charters revoked by sponsors (a local school board, state education agency, or university).

Early Promise

Evidence on the growth and outcomes of this relatively new movement has started to come in. The U.S. Department of Education's First Year Report, part of a four-year national study on charters, is based on interviews of 225 charter schools in 10 states (1997). Charters tend to be small (fewer than 200 students) and represent primarily new schools, though some schools have converted to charter status. Charter schools often tend to exist in urban locations, rather than rural.

This study found enormous variation among states. Charter schools tended to be somewhat more racially diverse, and to enroll slightly fewer students with special needs and limited-English-proficient students than the average schools in their state. The most common reasons for founding charters were to pursue an educational vision and gain autonomy.

"Charter schools are havens for children who had bad educational experiences elsewhere," according to a Hudson Institute in survey of students, teachers, and parents from fifty charters in ten states." More than 60 percent of the parents said charter schools are better than their children's previous schools in terms of teaching quality, individual attention from teachers, curriculum, discipline, parent involvement, and academic standards. Most teachers reported feeling empowered and professionally fulfilled (Vanourek and others 1997).

Recent Findings

On August 16, 2004, the Department of Education released a great number of reports without public announcement. Buried in the mountains of data was the first national comparison of test scores among children in charter schools and regular public schools. These results, from a study of six-thousand fourth grade pupils in 2003, showed charter school students performing worse in both mathematics and reading than comparable students in regular public schools. This study may have been buried to avoid negative publicity, since the Bush administration has been a strong supporter of charter schools.

These results were the most comprehensive so far, holding constant such factors as race, neighborhood, and income. Many conservative foundations had requested the study, hoping that the results would show gains for charter schools. Chester Finn, the president of one such foundation, admitted, "The scores are low, dismayingly low." One possible explanation is that enrollment in charter schools selects for students who were having academic trouble. A number of prominent research experts called into question the usefulness of the findings and the largely unrigorous media coverage that they received. At a December 2004 workshop held by the National Assessment Governing Board (NAGB) to discuss the findings of the 2003 National Assessment of Educational Progress (NAEP) pilot study on charter schools, government officials urged charter opponents and proponents alike to use caution in making "sweeping" conclusions from the NAEP report. NAGB Chairman Darvin Winick called attention to what he called the "fine print" of the study—that is, "one snapshot in time cannot determine the achievement of students."

A Harvard study also released in December 2004 that included 99 percent of all elementary charter school students found that they performed favorably in both math and reading compared to similar students in nearby conventional public schools, and that the longer the charter school had been in operation, the more favorably its students compared.

Other Problems

Nearly all charter schools face implementation obstacles, but newly created schools are most vulnerable. Most new charters are plagued by resource limitations, particularly inadequate startup funds.

Although charter advocates recommend the schools control all per-pupil funds, in reality they rarely receive as much funding as other public schools. They generally lack access to funding for facilities and special program funds distributed on a district basis (Bierlein and Bateman 1996). Sometimes private businesses and foundations, such as the Ameritech Corporation in Michigan and the Annenburg Fund in California, provide support (Jenkins and Dow). Congress and the President allocated $80 million to support charter-school activities in fiscal year 1998, up from $51 million in 1997.

Charter schools sometimes face opposition from local boards, state education agencies, and unions. Many educators are concerned that charter schools might siphon off badly needed funds for regular schools. The American Federation of Teachers urges that charter schools adopt high standards, hire only certified teachers, and maintain teachers' collective-bargaining rights. Also, some charters feel they face unwieldy regulatory barriers.

According to Bierlein and Bateman, the odds are stacked against charter schools. There may be too few strong-law states to make a significant difference. Educators who are motivated enough to create and manage charter schools could easily be burnt out by a process that demands increased accountability while providing little professional assistance.

Policy and Practice

As more states join the movement, there is increasing speculation about upcoming legislation. In an innovation-diffusion study surveying education policy experts in fifty states, Michael Mintrom and Sandra Vergari (1997) found that charter legislation is more readily considered in states with a policy entrepreneur, poor test scores, Republican legislative control, and proximity to other charter-law states. Legislative enthusiasm, gubernatorial support, interactions with national authorities, and use of permissive charter-law models increase the chances for adopting stronger laws. Seeking union support and using restrictive models presage adoption of weaker laws.

The threat of vouchers, wavering support for public education, and bipartisan support for charters has led some unions to start charters themselves. Several AFT chapters, such as those in Houston and Dallas, have themselves started charters. The National Education Association has allocated $1.5 million to help members start charter schools. Charters offer teachers a brand of empowerment, employee ownership, and governance that might be enhanced by union assistance (Nathan).

Professor Frank Smith, of Columbia University Teachers College, sees the charter-school movement as a chance to involve entire communities in redesigning all schools and converting them to "client-centered, learning cultures" (1997). He favors the Advocacy Center Design process used by state-appointed Superintendent Laval Wilson to transform four failing New Jersey schools. Building stronger communities via newly designed institutions may prove more productive than charters' typical "free-the-teacher-and-parent" approach.

President Bush's No Child Left Behind Act also promoted charter schools. Is it unclear whether recent test results will affect the enacting of future legislation? A Pennsylvania legislator who voted to create charter schools, State Rep. Mark B. Cohen of Philadelphia, said that "Charter schools offer increased flexibility to parents and administrators, but at a cost of reduced job security to school personnel. The evidence to date shows that the higher turnover of staff undermines school performance more than it enhances it, and that the problems of urban education are far too great for enhanced managerial authority to solve in the absence of far greater resources of staff, technology, and state of the art buildings."

TUITION VOUCHERS FOR RELIGIOUS SCHOOLS

SUCCESS STORY: Yolanda Richardson, 35, mother of Shada, 17, and Victor, 15; Milwaukee

DILEMMA: After growing up in Milwaukee's Hillside housing project, Yolanda Richardson knew she wanted a better future for her two children. So she joined the Navy, serving as a deck seaman in the Persian Gulf while her mother took care of the kids. When her tour of duty ended, she wanted to move Shada, then 6, Victor, then 4, and her mom to Norfolk, Virginia, "where Black people had good schools and opportunities to excel." But because of her job, her mom wouldn't relocate, and Yolanda, a single parent, had to return to Milwaukee.

Her children's schools broke her heart. The classrooms teamed with unruly students and harried instructors barely went through the motions of teaching. "It was a disaster," Yolanda recalls. She knew her kids would languish, as she had, in a school system in which most educators "would not give you a chance if you grew up around them."

SOLUTION: When seats failed to open up at a top high school, Yolanda opted for Milwaukee's Parental Choice program. It began in 1990 after the state of Wisconsin saw a drop in achievement so staggering it declared an emergency. The program provides vouchers, which often cover full tuition, to low-income students who wish to attend private or religious schools.

Parental Choice enrolls 11,621 of the system's 105,000 students. Nationwide, public-school students in five states—Maine, Vermont, Ohio, Wisconsin and Florida—can receive tax-supported scholarships or tuition vouchers to attend private or religious schools.

The $5,500 Yolanda received for each child through the program made it possible for her kids to attend Messmer High School, the top-tier Catholic school nearby. Initially Shada, then 15, and Victor, 13, balked at the thought of a dress code. "You need an education more than you need to worry about what to wear," countered their mom. And there were other hurdles: placement exams, interviews, checks on grades. But the children were willing to give it a try. They started in fall 2001 and soon blossomed academically, athletically and socially.

WHY IT WORKS FOR HER: Yolanda has seen the positive effects Messmer's strict but caring teachers and firm disciplinary code have had on her children. At first Victor seemed more focused on perfecting his jump shot than his academic skills. Then one day he was caught in the locker room with some other students who were reportedly shooting dice, and he was asked to leave Messmer, though he maintained he hadn't participated. After finding himself back in regular high school, he quickly realized what he'd lost and vowed to work hard, earn top grades and return to Messmer. He did. Back as a sophomore this fall, Victor is a star off court and on. His sister Shada, also a sophomore (because she had been kept back in grade school), has a 3.6 GPA and is a leader in her Bible-studies group. "Don't let your surroundings predict your future," Yolanda often tells them.

MILITARY ACADEMY SCHOOLS

Chicago has more student military programs than any city in the United States. In addition to the five schools, Chicago is home to 33 high schools—based Junior Reserve Officer Training Corps (JROTC) programs. [21]

Supporters say that the programs teach kids discipline. Not everyone thinks these schools are a good idea, though. They say public schools shouldn't groom kids for the U.S. military under the guise of education. [22]

Chicago's military high schools instill good work ethics and discipline in students, says the chief executive officer of the Chicago Public Schools, (now Secretary of Education) Arne Duncan.

"[Military school is] getting these kids ready for college or whatever they want to do after high school. Our focus is just getting them as well prepared as we can . . . for the rest of their lives," Duncan told Current Events. [23]

All but two of the schools—Chicago and Carver military academies—are too new to gauge how well they are performing, Duncan adds, but he's confident that they will turn out kids who score high on tests and go on to college. "[The graduation rate and test scores] are pretty good; they aren't as strong as we would like them to be, but they are going up," he says. Regardless, Duncan adds, demand from both parents and prospective students are high for the schools. Last year 7,500 applicants applied for the 700 freshman slots in the five schools.[24]

Others say Chicago's military schools and JROTC programs help average students thrive in school. "We intend to use the academies to take students who perform in the middle range and use the military model to enhance their . . . education," Army Lt. Col. Rick Mills, who oversees the Chicago JROTC program, told the Chicago Tribune.[25]

Too Much Military

Those who oppose the schools and programs, however, think they are just ploys to get more kids into the military. "Chicago Public Schools should be in the business of educating children, not finding ways to indoctrinate them into the military," Brian Roa told the Chicago Tribune.[26] He's a Chicago science teacher who is a member of the National Network Opposing Militarization of Youth.

Darlene Gramigna of the American Friends Service Committee agrees. She says the schools' educational policies are too focused on the military. "So much of education has taken a military focus . . . .

[In these schools] it's a different curriculum. It's the history of wars, and it's field trips to naval academies," Gramigna told Current Events.[27]

Kids don't need to practice countless drills to learn about discipline, Gramigna says. "I would like to believe that you could teach leadership and discipline in a variety of ways," she adds.28

Chicago Public Schools opened its fifth military high school in the fall of 2008—the Marine Military Academy. In 2009, a sixth school—an Air Force academy—will open as well. Chicago will be the only city with schools dedicated to the Army, Navy, Air Force, and Marines.

The National Defense Act of 1916 created the Junior Reserve Officer Training Corps (JROTC). Under the act, high schools receive federal funding and loans of military equipment as well as military instructors to provide three hours of military instruction per week. A school has to maintain at least 100 students over the age of 14 in the program.

The 1964 ROTC Vitalization Act expanded the program. About 500,000 students are involved in high school military programs across the United States, according to the Chicago Tribune.[29]

When a new military school opens in Chicago, it starts with only freshmen and then adds a new class each year.

THE CURSE OF UNIONS
EASY PICKINGS—EFFECTS OF TENURE

Teachers' unions and other groups contend that draining money and motivated students from struggling schools will only destroy public education.

Few public officials are better paid—or less accountable—than school administrators.

Most Buffalo school administrators are former teachers who have learned that there is good money to be made running a poor district. School officials accounted for 81 of the city's 100 highest paid administrators in 1996-97.

How much better paid are school administrators than their city government counterparts? Seventy-five made more in 1996-97 than Mayor Anthony Masiello, who ranked 91st overall among city administrators. The schools' top budget official earned nearly $24,000 more than the mayor's chief number cruncher. Seventeen principals made more than the police commissioner, including four who pulled down more than $100,000. Even the School Board's secretary made more than most of the city government's top administrators; even though of the $63,189 she earned, much of it in overtime, and her pay topped those of the commissioners of parks, streets, and community development.

Sixty-five percent of the administrators in the city who made over $65,000 work for the schools. In 1996-97, 191 school administrators were paid more than $65,000, including 40 who earned more than $80,000. The Superintendent topped the list. His $135,000 salary makes him the city's highest paid public official. Benefits for city school administrators are vastly superior to those of the mayor's management staff. School administrators who retired the summer of 1996, for example, walked away with an average of $49,940 in early retirement incentives and compensation for unused sick time; department heads in the city get nothing when they leave.

While the city high school principals' pay—$94,486—is higher than those in the suburbs, most of their students' academic performance is not. Most city high schools are at the bottom of the achievement ladder among schools. Student performance is not tied to principals' pay.

The district's administrators rank among the best paid managers in city government—and the least accountable. They're rarely evaluated. And forget about demotions or dismissals. All but a handful have what amounts to lifetime job security. Even assistant superintendents are members of a union and expected to supervise and, if necessary, discipline fellow members of their union. The situation in Buffalo is worse than in many other districts, but in many ways it typifies the entrenched bureaucrats found in school systems throughout the nation. "I think the public education system is about as unaccountable as anything the human mind has conceived," says Joe Nathan, director of the Center for School Change at the University of Minnesota. "What's happened in Buffalo and a number of other places is that the preferences of adults have become more important than the needs of children. Our school systems are fundamentally set up as employment agencies rather than educational institutions."

Buffalo City Comptroller Joel Giambra complains that there's no link between the high salaries being earned by school administrators and the performance of their students. The district usually evaluates new administrators before they're granted permanent status after three years on the job, but the evaluation criteria is fuzzy, and it's rare that anyone is turned down. A curriculum audit conducted in March 1997 by a team of national experts found a haphazard and incomplete evaluation process. Auditors randomly pulled the files of 40 administrators and found 24 had no evaluations. The grading system used on the remaining 16 was generous. Administrators were given the highest grade possible 87 percent of the time and unsatisfactory ratings were issued in less than 1 percent of the categories in which they were graded. "It's been 24 years since my last evaluation," one administrator told auditors. "There isn't an evaluation system after administrators become tenured," another said.

When the new superintendent came aboard, he inherited a management staff of about 220, including assistant superintendents, directors and supervisors who work out of the central office, and principals and assistant principals working in schools. He had the authority to replace only six of the 220: three associate superintendents, two special assistants focused on budget and media relations, and a labor negotiator. Removing any of the others would have required the district to prove incompetence or misconduct. Simply doing a mediocre job, or the emergence of someone better suited for the position, are not sufficient cause to remove or demote a school administrator in Buffalo.

Unions have such a stranglehold that the superintendent couldn't even hire his own confidential secretary. Union work rules dictate who he got and, unlike the situation in most workplaces, she is a union member and not considered confidential management. In contrast, the mayor not only can hire his own secretary, but also commissioners, deputy commissioners and a host of other managers. In all, the mayor has control over 42 management positions that are exempt from union representation. Masiello describes the district's lack of management rights as "an obstacle." "Management needs to have the rights and flexibility to manage and hold people accountable," he said.

But the times are changing elsewhere. A growing number of states and school districts are holding principals and other school administrators more accountable by regularly evaluating their performance and in some cases eliminating tenure. While tenure for principals is embedded in New York state law, it is being challenged around the country. Massachusetts, Georgia, North Carolina and Oregon have stripped' their principals of tenure in recent years, reducing to 16 the number of states that provide principals with tenure.

The Chicago school system, considered one of the nation's most troubled districts in the '80s, has been the most aggressive in holding administrators accountable. "Linking job security to student performance has been a cornerstone of efforts to improve the district," says G. Alfred Hess, director of the Center for Urban School Policy at Northwestern University and an observer to the Chicago reform movement. "We saw principals' lifetime tenure as one of the major problems in getting school improvement to happen," he also says. "The leadership was not accountable for the performance of the kids."

The Illinois State Legislature enacted reforms in 1988 and 1995. Councils consisting primarily of parents have gained greater control over school budgets and can hire and fire principals. The mayor appoints the school board and hires the top five central office administrators. The teachers union's power has been reduced and principals lost their tenure altogether. As a result, ineffective teachers and administrators at poorly performing schools can be fired. "The difference is night and day," Hess says. "Previously, principals understood their main job was to make sure their school didn't get into the news, except for something wonderful. And as long as they kept their school out of trouble, nobody cared what happened. Nobody ever got fired because the kids didn't learn. Now the primary question about the performance of school officials is whether their kids are learning or not."

The reforms are paying off. The percentage of students reading at national norms climbed from 24 to 35 percent from 1990 to 1998. "I would say 85 percent of the credit for changes in student achievement relate to the ability to change the principal at the school," Hess says. "Effective principals make or break improving schools."

"If you want to improve student achievement, you have to tie job security to whether kids are learning more. Otherwise educators' prejudice about the ability of low-income and minority kids to learn gets in the way of change," Hess says. "If you can say, `It's not my fault, it's the kids I have to teach,' you're not going to get much change in those schools. But if people say, `Your job security depends on whether kids in your classes are learning,' then you have a whole different lever for change."

AFTER SCHOOL PROGRAMS-

A Missed Opportunity

In too many schools today, 3 p.m. marks a daily missed opportunity to meet the tougher achievement demands placed on students and school districts.

For many children, it's when learning effectively stops and when opportunities for inappropriate behaviors line up to take their place. It's when many parents worry, rightly, that their children aren't sufficiently supervised. It's when community, youth, arts and law enforcement groups could /should become potential allies with the school district in assisting to maintain children on track and learning.

Ironically, it's the hour when many of the school district's investments in learning resources and facilities sit idle.

But in more and more school districts around the nation, it has become the time of day for new and creative learning opportunities, offered in settings where children are supervised by professional educators and community partners. By most assessments, today's after-school programs make a positive difference in the lives of students and improve the climate for school and district success.

Accordingly, after-school programs are very popular with the public. A series of annual voter surveys conducted by the Afterschool Alliance shows public support consistently running in the 90 percent range, with 76 percent of voters even going so far as to say they'd be willing to pay additional taxes if more after-school programs resulted.[30]

Multiple Effects

It is perhaps little surprising that those in the business of creating more after-school opportunities believe the current flat-lining of after-school funding is a very bad mistake. To advocates and practitioners, the benefits from after-school programs are in plain evidence, and study after study by independent academics have demonstrated their value. Researchers have examined the impact of programs on students' achievement, social interaction and safety. They've looked at short- and long-term effects. They've examined a broad variety of programs in a range of settings. Results vary somewhat from program to program, but the weight of the research evidence tells us that after-school, done right, lives up to its promise.

To hear Arne Duncan, than CEO of the Chicago Public Schools, (now Secretary of the Department of Education) tell it at a May 2003 press briefing: "If you look at results—and we do have to be bottom-line oriented—our test scores jumped to all-time highs, our mobility rate dropped to its lowest point ever, our truancy rate dropped to its lowest point ever, our graduation rate is at an all-time high.[31]

"For the first time ever, we have 8th graders beating national norms; that has never happened before. In a district where 85 percent of our students live below the poverty line, that was a huge real and symbolic accomplishment. Children's minds don't stop at 3 p.m., and neither should their learning. So their schools and community partners should not stop teaching.[32]

According to the California Department of Education, an evaluation of the statewide found significant improvements in achievement among the most high-risk students," as well as "a direct relationship between gains in math and amount of participation in the program."[33]

Students who participated for 7.5 months or more demonstrated improvements in math scores that were more than 2.5 times those found statewide. School attendance also improved, especially among students having the highest number of absences prior to participating in the program.[34]

Free After School Learning Centers

Studies have found the most critical children's minds don't stop at 3 p.m., and neither should their learning.

A critical time for child's educational development is between 3:00 p.m. when kids return home from school, and 6:00 p.m. when the parents arrive home from work. It is critical because that's the time when they should be doing homework assignments, in preparation for the next school day.

For many children, it's when learning effectively stops and when opportunities for inappropriate behaviors line up to take their place.

It's when many parents worry, rightly, that their children aren't sufficiently supervised. It's when community, youth, arts and law enforcement groups could become potential allies with the school district in helping keep children on track and learning. In more and more school districts around the nation, it has become the time of day for new and creative learning opportunities, offered in settings where children are supervised by professional educators and community partners. By most assessments, today's after-school programs make a positive difference in the lives of students and improve the climate for school and district success.

With today's increasingly rigorous academic standards, many students need additional learning time. The public understands as much. In the 2004 Phi Delta Kappa/Gallup Poll, 94 percent of those surveyed support increasing instructional time. At the same time, rapidly changing workplace demands mean that many working parents need additional help during after-school time to keep children on track.

So it is fair to wonder whether we are on the verge of missing a unique, even historic, opportunity to fill the hours immediately following the end of the school day with a treasure chest of academically enriching activities and expanded learning opportunities, provided by these programs.

To hear Arne Duncan, CEO of the Chicago Public Schools, tell it at a May 2003 press briefing: "If you look at results—and we do have to be bottom-line oriented—our test scores jumped to all-time highs, our mobility rate dropped to its lowest point ever, our truancy rate dropped to its lowest point ever, our graduation rate is at an all-time high.

"For the first time ever, we have 8th graders beating national norms; that has never happened before. In a district where 85 percent of our students live below the poverty line, that was a huge real and symbolic accomplishment. Duncan and other school leaders see after-school programs as an opportunity to meet escalating state requirements and No Child Left Behind standards. The framework for fixing what ails public education reaches beyond the school system's immediate resources to involve the broader community—volunteers, sponsoring businesses, the faith community, civic organizations and the philanthropic community.

Well-structured after-school programs effectively expand learning time for students. Children get individual tutoring along with lessons and activities that reinforce the day's class work and the night's homework. Looking down the road, Huron Valley, Mich., Superintendent Robert O'Brien, who was his state's 2003 Superintendent of the Year, points to the significant long-range benefits from after-school. "Research shows that children involved in sports or other after-school activities do better academically, socially and emotionally," he told the Detroit News in December 2004. "They are also less likely to become involved in risky behaviors such as drugs."

Noting that the middle school years play an important role in the transition from child to young adult, "this transition is made easier if students learn problem solving, teamwork, leadership and experience new things," O'Brien said.

A Resource Question

Of course, school districts would be significantly assisted in their efforts to expand after-school by an increase in funding for the federal 21st Century Community Learning Centers. No Child Left Behind authorized $2 billion for the current year, but Congress and the president have provided only $1 billion of that. Separately, states could provide a big boost by including after-school funding in their state school finance formulas. Educators are well advised to advocate for such increases.

That said, however, many school district leaders have found a solution to the funding problem in capitalizing on their own resources to leverage the involvement of community, law-enforcement, youth, parks and recreation, and faith, cultural and civic organizations to help sponsor and deliver quality after-school programs. District facilities, classrooms, computer and language labs, libraries, and arts and sports facilities keep students learning after 3 p.m.

Comprehensive Education Structure

Educating Black children should be undertaken in a comprehensive way. It should begin with programs like Head Start which would give economically challenged kids a fair opportunity to develop learning skills in their early years.

School choice, which would include programs such as Same Sex schools, Job-oriented, Industrial Arts/Technical schools, funded choice schools, and a vibrant Special Need programs, are a necessity if black kids are to succeed.

It can be argued that school districts are always financially challenged to provide basic services, let alone trying to provide the previously mentioned programs. With that said, a creative look at the available Federal funding such as No Child Left Behind, Faith Based Initiative, etc. is one possible direction that a dedicated education structure should peruse as funding sources.

As previously stated, one of the most critical learning periods for most kids is between 3:00p.m. and 6:00p.m. Additionally, since some kids don't have the home environment conducive to productive after school studying, a comprehensive after school study program is vital. Quality after school programs have proven successful in reducing poor next day class performance in most kids, thus every effort should be made to develop and institute such programs.

Feed The Children

The most difficult time for large segments of the black population is after 3p.m, they will go to bed hungry. Sometime, for a lot of disadvantaged kids, the only meal that these kids will get is in school. It is impossible for a hungry kid to do homework assignments because they are hungry. The lucky kids attend a school that has a breakfast and lunch program. In most cases, they will get a snack in the morning, with lunch later. Often these are the only meals that they will get during the day. How can kids be developmentally productive when they are hungry?

There should be a commitment to, at the very lease, provide an after school take—home meal for those kids who would like to have them. This is not rocket science, they provide lunches for prisoners with court appearances every day. The resources are already in place to accomplish this task through the school cafeteria staff present at most schools. It would only require increasing the food allotment at the relevant schools, and a possible increase of (1) additional staff. It is reasonable to realize an increase in student performance as result of this vital gesture. I know from personnel experience how important this would be to a lot of kids.

THE INVALUABLE ROLE OF HBCUs

The National Black College and University system should not be forgotten in this equation. Black Colleges and Universities should be one of the first choices for most black kids.

We spend too much time comparing ourselves to white folks instead of comparing ourselves to the task of educating ALL Black kids.

Redefining the American High School

American high schools were not designed to prepare all of our young people to be successful citizens in today's challenging world.

The Problem

Due to today's demanding job market, some kind of education after high school is vital—whether it's a four-year college, community college, technical school, or a formal apprenticeship. Yet most students leave high school without the necessary skills for college or a living wage job.

Nearly three out of 10 public high school students fail to graduate, and close to half of all African-American (44 percent) and Hispanic students (48 percent) leave high school without a diploma.[35]

Only 23 percent of African Americans and one-fifth of Hispanics graduate from high school prepared for a four-year college.[36]

Only three of five college freshmen will earn a B.A. within six years; for minority and low-income students, the number is closer to half.[37]

The Consequences For The Nation's Civic And Economic Health

Nearly 40 percent of high school graduates feel inadequately prepared for college or the workplace.[38]

Colleges and employers are demanding the same core knowledge and skills.[39] Over half of professors (54 percent) and nearly three-fifths of employers (58 percent) do not agree with the statement that high school graduates have the skills necessary for college or work respectively.[40]

The more education a person has, the more likely it is he or she will be employed.[41] Among high school dropouts ages 16 to 24, nearly half are jobless and a third receive some type of government assistance.[42] Over a quarter (28 percent) of college freshmen must take remedial courses.[43]

By 2020, the nation may face a shortage of 14 million workers with college-level skills.[44]

High school dropouts will earn more than $1 million less over a lifetime than college graduates.[11]

Blacks Have Low Educational Attainment Rates

There is an often repeated claim that "there are more black men in prison than in college." Besides being statistically wrong, 45 it also bolsters the second biggest myth about black Americans: it is a myth that blacks on the whole have low educational attainment rates. While there are statistics that point to less black men graduating college or lower college graduation rates. The absolute numbers of blacks attending college has increased over time and continues to increase.[46]

Historically Black Colleges and Universities (HBCUs) are institutions founded primarily for the education of African-Americans, although their charters were not exclusionary. Most HBCUs are 50 to 100 years old; the oldest HBCU dates back to 1837. Of the 105 HBCUs, 17 HBCUs have land-grant status.[47]

About 214,000 or 16 percent of all African-American higher education students in the nation are enrolled at HBCUs, which comprise 3 percent of all colleges and universities nation-wide.[48]

The National Association for Equal Opportunity in Higher Education (NAFEO) is a professional association that represents the nation's HBCUs.

Summary of Interesting Facts about HBCUs

4-Year Public	40	38.09%
4-Year Private	49	46.66%
2-Year Public	11	10.48%
2-Year Private	5	4.76%
Total	105	

HBCU African Americans Black Diamonds

Black Americans have a unique, yet undeveloped, educational opportunity to build an educated middle class in America. Through the proper managing, resourcing, and the demanding of education excellence the HBCU network can become a very special educational experience for black kids. Where else can you have the pride that results from watching the FAM marching band?

The HBCU network consists of 105 colleges and universities. Some are Land Grant; some are private, while others are state funded. In most instances they are underfunded and mismanaged. The management of these institutions is usually performed by educators, not business trained and experienced managers.

The academic credibility of some institutions is, in some instances, not competitive with most white institutions. This perception has been fostered by some in society with an agenda of diminishing the value of an education *from HBCU. There is truth that Howard University is not competitive with Harvard University. The question that should be asked is, why? What ever the reason is, it should be resolved. There is now a cadre of skilled, experienced, professional black managers that should feel challenged to, after their current careers are over, help build one of the most valued black community resources, the HBCU system. There are former black CEO's of Fortune 500 companies that can bring a wealth of knowledge for setting up efficient management systems, financial resource development systems, and investment portfolio development. Recruiting retired senior corporate managers to form an HBCU management consulting structure for these institutions would began to bring some order.*

For a variety of reasons, this resource has been allowed to fail many black kids. The problems are not always educational, they are mostly resource management. The HBCU system was, at one time, suppose to be exclusively for black kids. It was supposed to our place to educate our kids.

List of HBCU by State

ALABAMA
Alabama State University
Alabama A&M University
Tuskegee University

ARKANSAS
University of Arkansas Pine Bluff

DELAWARE
Delaware State University

DISTRICT of COLUMBIA
Howard University
University of the District of Columbia

FLORIDA
Bethune Cookman College
Edward Waters
Florida A&M University

GEORGIA
Clark Atlanta University
Morehouse College
Morris Brown College
Spelman College

ILLINOIS
Malcolm X College

LOUISIANA
Grambling State University
Southern University

MARYLAND
Bowie State University
Coppin State College
Morgan State University
University of Maryland Eastern Shore

MISSISSIPPI
Alcorn State
Jackson State University
Tougaloo College

NORTH CAROLINA
Fayetteville State University
North Carolina A&T University
Saint Augustine College

JAMES C. ROLLINS

Shaw University
Winston Salem State University

OHIO
Central State University

SOUTHCAROLINA
Claflin University

TEXAS
Prairie View A&M University
Texas Southern University

TENNESSEE
Fisk University
LeMoyne Owen College
Tennessee State University

VIRGINIA
Hampton University
Norfolk State University

4

SCHOOL-TO-CAREER

Possible Solution

The current high school model is geared toward preparation for a college degree, with little emphasis on vocational skills training. Below is a copy of a Organized Labor brochure in support of School-to-Career program. [44]

Get Connected to School–to–Career

This Quick Guide for Organized Labor is designed to help increase participation in School-to-Career efforts and to help you get started if you are not yet involved. It provides teachers, employers, administrators, and other partners in School-to-Career an "inside look" on Labor's values and the roles we can play in local School-to-Career activities. Work is a big part of shaping who we are and how we contribute to our families and communities. Still, many of our young people leave school unprepared to enter the workforce and ill equipped to explore career options on their own. How can we best introduce young people to the opportunities of future careers and the contributions of organized labor? The School to Work Opportunities Act of 1994, backed by the AFL-CIO and teachers' unions, supports state and local partnerships of Labor, educators, employers, parents and community organizations to develop School-to-Career educational systems.

What is School-to-Career?

School-to-Career is an approach to education based on proven concepts. It is based on the idea that if students understand the relevancy of their academic studies and if their classroom learning is linked to future goals and careers, these students are likely to achieve higher performance in school and graduate with significantly improved knowledge and skills.

School-to-Career activities provide a better education for ALL students, whether they choose to attend college or move into the workforce. These activities may include curriculum enrichment (creating lessons that are current and relevant), worksite tours, classroom presentations on career and training opportunities, internships, and direct interaction with workers in real work situations. For those young people not fully engaged in their academic educational system, it encourages learning linked to future work and career efforts. The connection between the classroom and the world of work increases students' motivation and academic achievement, while better preparing our young people for their adult lives.

Why Should Labor Be Involved in School-to-Career?

Labor has been involved in School-to-Career (or School-to-Work) nationwide for many years. The logic is simple: we do the work and we are in the best position to share and pass on to younger people the "real stories"—life lessons about work places and relationships as well as the actual skills necessary to be successful in a particular career.

School-to-Career is an opportunity for union members to prepare the next generation for the world of work and help students explore a wide range of occupations and careers. We hope that many of these students will eventually become union brothers and sisters.

Organized Labor Makes Significant Contributions to Successful School-to-Career Systems

Organized Labor can be of substantial help in developing a comprehensive School-to-Career curriculum that conveys in a meaningful way all aspects of an industry showcasing those viewpoints of the workers performing the actual work. This might include the social interaction of work, the benefits of certain jobs, necessary skills for success and the long-term impact of working in a certain field.

Unions also operate apprenticeship training centers that offer preparation and hands-on learning to introduce students to the education, skills, and abilities needed to enter into registered trades and crafts apprenticeships. These apprenticeships require desire, certain aptitudes, a commitment of time, and considerable study but can all lead to high-wage, high-skill employment opportunities.

Additional contributions organized Labor makes to successful School-to-Career systems include: Unions represent millions of front-line workers that can be called upon to support young people in job shadowing, mentoring, internships, apprenticeships and other work-based learning opportunities.

Unions have direct links to employers in a wide variety of occupational areas and can play a key role in facilitating employer involvement in School-to-Career activities.

Unions can play an important role in linking school-based learning with on-the-job training (OJT).

Unions are at the forefront of education and advocacy for workers' health and safety protection.

Unions can be instrumental in securing additional funding for local School-to-Career Partnerships and activities.

Organized Labor Benefits From Participation in School-to-Career

School-to-Career is a proven winner in education reform efforts. We have a self-interest as well as responsibility for providing young people with the best education possible; young people are the future of our Labor movement as well as society at large. By being active partners, we build stronger educational systems in our communities. As members of organized Labor, we expect every job to be done well and that the people performing the job are compensated fairly, work in a safe environment, and are treated with dignity and respect. Young people are well served to learn and understand our values. Labor's involvement in School-to-Career is an opportunity for us Through School-to-Career; Labor introduces awareness of the contributions and to communicate this message directly.

The School-to-Work Opportunities Act: It's the Law . . . It's important to know that statutes and laws mandate the inclusion of Labor in the design and implementation of School-to-Career systems. These laws provide safeguards for the rights of young workers in School-to-Career. These measures of inclusion and protection reinforce the important role Labor plays in the overall School-to-Career effort.

The School to Work Opportunities Act of 1994: 25 Highest-Paying Jobs for High School Grads

While nearly all of the highest paying jobs in America require a bachelor's degree or higher, good-paying occupations still exist that require only work experience or on-the-job-training.

Air traffic controllers had median hourly wages of $51.73 and median annual wages of $107,600 in 2005, making it the highest paid occupation that requires only work experience or on-the-job-training, according to the Bureau of Labor Statistics.

Air traffic controllers have seen their wages rise from 2005 to 2007. In July 2007, air traffic controllers earned a median of $120,842 in annual wages, according to HR.BLR.com's Salary Center.[2]

Among the 25 highest paid occupations overall, air traffic controller is the only one with no requirement for a bachelor's degree or higher.

Among occupations requiring only work experience or on-the-job-training, managers and industrial production managers are the second and third highest paying jobs.

The following are the 25 highest paying occupations requiring only work experience or on-the-job training:

	Occupation	Median Wages 2013	
		Hourly	Annual
1	Air Traffic Controllers	$51.73	$107,600
2	Managers, All Other	$38.06	$79,200
3	Industrial Production Managers	$36.34	$75,600
4	Transportation, Storage, and Distribution Managers	$33.23	$69,100
5	Nuclear Power Reactor Operators	$31.84	$66,200
6	First-Line Supervisors/Managers of Police and Detectives	$31.52	$65,600
7	First-Line Supervisors/Managers of Non-Retail Sales Workers	$29.79	$62,000
8	First-Line Supervisors/Managers of Fire Fighting and Prevention Workers	$29.25	$60,800
9	Sales Representatives, Wholesale and Manufacturing, Technical and Scientific Products	$29.21	$60,800
10	Gaming Managers	$28.82	$59,900
11	Elevator Installers and Repairers	$28.46	$59,200
12	Power Distributors and Dispatchers	$28.44	$59,200
13	Real Estate Brokers	$27.49	$57,200
14	Detectives and Criminal Investigators	$26.82	$55,800
15	Locomotive Engineers	$26.69	$55,500
16	Railroad Conductors and Yardmasters	$25.98	$54,000
17	Power Plant Operators	$25.56	$53,200
18	Postmasters and Mail Superintendents	$25.34	$52,700
19	Cost Estimators	$25.01	$52,000
20	First-Line Supervisors/Managers of Mechanics, Installers, and Repairers	$24.99	$52,000
21	First-Line Supervisors/Managers of Construction Trades and Extraction Workers	$24.98	$52,000
22	Gas Plant Operators	$24.96	$51,900
23	Petroleum Pump System Operators, Refinery Operators, and Gaugers	$24.55	$51,100
24	Captains, Mates, and Pilots of Water Vessels	$24.49	$50,900
	Telecommunications Equipment Installers	$24.33	$50,600

On a daily basis young students in America are bombarded with the notion that you can only succeed in life if you have a post secondary education, a degree. To reinforce this notion, the educational system is primarily structured to accomplishing this goal. President Barack Obama, when speaking on education, constantly reinforces college as the only road to success in life. Those without the financial resource or the GPA are given few career options. In most instances, they give up because they have no interest in college. They are never told of, or prepared for all of the other great options out there such as vocational and technical career options.

In the earlier example of school to career, if properly executed, every student would have a path to becoming a productive, responsible adult after high school and, in many cases a college degree will become a viable later option because of financial stability. All of the previously mentioned jobs are export proof. These are infrastructure related, and can only be performed by the local labor force. These positions are also relative free of the fluctuations in the financial cycles. Subsequently, these education and career options should be made available to future students.

Currently, option and dream in today's environment is crushed, leaving only frustration, bad choices, and bad outcomes. The world might be designed by scholars, but it is built and maintained by technicians. Everyone should have a dream.

5

THE BLACK ECONOMY
BLING-BLING BROKE

The true story of wealth in the Black Community

Many individuals in the African American community are beginning to resent their conventional image as oppressed and economically disadvantaged. The raw numbers from the 1990 census show that African Americans made considerable economic and educational progress during the 1990s. The African American median household income grew fifteen percent between 1989 and 1999, compared with six percent for white families. The number of black-owned businesses increased by twenty-six percent from 1992 to 1997 compared with an overall seven percent increase for U.S. businesses. The net worth of African-American households grew to $1 trillion in 2001, but their growth in wealth was outpaced by that of other (ethnic group) households. Once again, we fall into the trap of comparing our progress to other ethnic groups, instead of the task, of growing wealth in the Black community.

As consumers, African Americans are one of the most targeted markets in modern times. We spend $571 billion annually on consumer goods—$270 billion more than a decade ago. While travel overall in the United States increased 1 percent between 1997 and 1999, the number of blacks traveling increased by 16 percent during that same period.

Blacks are economically depressed

Another common misperception of African-Americans is that on the whole, blacks are economically depressed in the United States. Once again, media crime reports from the 'ghetto,' hip-hop videos and gangsta rap do not show an accurate picture of black American wealth as a whole.

There is a projection that based on purchasing power alone, African-Americans eclipse all African countries and many emerging countries. African-American purchasing power is projected to exceed $1 trillion by 2012. This figure outstrips most other countries GDP. In fact, if African Americans were a country, it would be the tenth largest economy in the world today.9

The numerous portrayals in the mainstream media of black poverty and the seemingly "permanent" underclass do not reflect the overall wealth of African-Americans in the USA.

If the African-American portion of the US GDP was separated from the rest of the US GDP, itsTrillion would still eclipse most Third World and indeed many other "developed" countries, including Sweden.[10]

Not too many countries can match this amount, and blacks only have 13% of the US population.

Many other countries make do with less GDP, and with many more people. The true test for the future is the effective use of this massive wealth to achieve proper respect.

A recent report issued by the Boston College Center on Wealth and Philanthropy (CWP) projects that the wealth transfer from African-American households via estates in the 55-year period between 2001 and 2055 will range between $1.1 trillion to $3.4 trillion (in 2003 U.S. dollars).

"We did find, however, that the growth in wealth among younger African-Americans who grew up after civil rights legislation was in effect identical to that for Caucasians of the same age and this is a hopeful sign for African-American wealth in the future," said CWP Associate Director John Havens, who directed the study.

According to the report, income, wealth and charitable giving in the African-American community have risen rapidly in recent years. From 1992 through 2001, after adjustment for inflation, they report, both aggregate income and aggregate wealth for African-American households have risen at an annual rate of 4 percent and aggregate charitable giving has risen at an annual rate of 5 percent.

Focus: Economic Wellness for African Americans

"At the bottom of education, at the bottom of politics, even at the bottom of religion, there must be economic independence." (Booker T. Washington, ca. 1903).

A healthy community has financially stable residents. So, what if a community's residents are lacking "wellness"; meaning they lack the financial resources that contribute to a stabile community? For example, most are aware of the economic disparity related to black vs. white income. However, regardless of ethnic background, community economic wellness indicators are the same; household assets, local business enterprises, home ownership and community involvement.

The time is now, according to many financial specialists, to strengthen the economic well-being of African American communities. Brooke Stephens, well renowned author and lecturer has a 7-step prescription creating economic wellness for African Americans and the communities in which they live. The following are her suggested steps and supporting data from the Bureau of Census and other publications:

1. *Create a wealth-building plan.* African-American households increased 32% in median income between 1993 and 2000. However, net worth of blacks is one-fifth that of whites. A wealth building plan is a financial plan in which the major goal is to increase your household's net worth. This means practicing good money and credit management, setting goals, and understanding the bottom-line importance of asset building.

2. *Invest in your dream every payday.* Planning and saving must become an immutable rule of life. Start small, and then grow. Have different savings vehicles (from a piggy bank, cd's and savings accounts, to bonds) that are for different goals.

3. *Own your home.* Home ownership is one of the most powerful tools to creating wealth. It creates a stable community, grows personal assets, and creates leverage for seeking other economic opportunities. Forty-seven percent of blacks own their own home; compared to over 56% for whites. The value of whites homes are an average $26,000 higher than blacks.

4. *Invest in the stock market.* In order to increase net worth, blacks will need to understand how to select, invest and maintain a portfolio of stocks or mutual funds. It is really not

that hard to understand and there are many experts ready to assist.

5. *Ensure yourself and your dreams.* African Americans live an average of six years less than whites, illustrating the need for African Americans to understand how to protect their families and financial dreams. Plan for retirement, understand the need to make plans for long-term care, know the best of life insurance, and plan for death with a will.

6. *Own a business or invest in a business.* If African Americans want to participate in the great bounty of America's free-enterprise system, then more will have to join the ranks of being an entrepreneur. Choose a business that can give the greatest return. The number of Black-owned businesses grew more than all U.S. businesses. However, black-owned businesses represent 1% of the total receipts for all business. This is partly due to the fact that these businesses are in the service industry, which traditionally reaps lower profits.

7. *Maximize your human resources.* Lastly, Ms. Stephens states, "For various reasons, African Americans have historically devalued and underused their intellectual, physical and spiritual resources." Blacks must understand how to maximize their human capital by improving their professional skills to increase their earning power, insisting that their children get a good education and becoming an active volunteer in their communities, places of worship and organizations.

There are many reasons why African-Americans may not be economically well, and getting well is not an easy pill to swallow. However, trying at least some of the remedies offered by Ms. Stephens can create economic wellness for individuals, their household and their community.

Keys to Black Empowerment

Black people are 12.7 percent of the population of the United States. We earn 8 percent of the income, but own just 3 percent of the wealth. Roughly, $2 trillion in assets is held by American households. Why is it that many African Americans have not experienced the same prosperity of many other consumers who took advantage of low mortgage rates to significantly increase their wealth?

When you look at some statistics, it's easy to see why there are some concerns that too many blacks are bling-bling broke.

According to Target Market News, which specializes in tracking African American marketing, media and consumer behavior, blacks spend more per capita than whites on many food, clothing and entertainment products and services.

Many point to the company's survey to criticize black spending. For example, blacks spend about $22 billion of their income on apparel products and services and almost $29 billion on automobiles.

Black households had a GDP of $679 billion in earned income in 2004, an increase of 3.5 percent over the $656 billion earned in 2003. A better way to appreciate that is to compare it in the following way. In 2005, the GDP for Argentina was 483.5 billion, South Africa 491.4 billion, Poland 463 billion. Black households had a GDP value higher than most countries in the world. If you use the overall earned income figure, it doesn't appear as if blacks are spending wisely.

On a household basis, the annual median income of blacks in 2004 was just $30,134, according to the U.S. Census Bureau. Asian households had the highest median income ($57,518). The median income for non-Hispanic white households was $48,977. For Hispanic households, it was $34,241.

But the fact is that a great deal of black spending is on necessities such as health care. The uninsured rate in 2004 was 11.3 percent for non-Hispanic whites but almost 20 percent for blacks. Meanwhile, African Americans, several studies have shown, are unfairly charged higher interest rates for big-ticket consumer items such as cars.

One of the keys to prosperity is homeownership.

While blacks spend $110 billion on housing, only 48 percent of black households owned their own home compared with 75.7 percent for white households, according to Census figures for the fourth quarter of 2005. In fact, African American homeownership declined one percentage point from the fourth quarter of 2004. That number should be going up, not down. (Overall homeownership declined as well, from 69.2 percent down to 69 percent.)

Own a home, and you have an asset that can boost your net worth. You can—as many people do—also use the equity you have in the home, meaning the difference between the mortgage balance and the home's current value, to bail yourself out of debt trouble or borrow to send your children to college or pay for a wedding or help them with a down payment on their first home.

In an effort to satisfy the low rate of home ownership, blacks embarked on a home buy frenzy in the early 2000's. The mortgage markets appear to be more responsive the minority barrower. Ultimately, what prove to be true was that financial opportunist/predator saw an opportunity to prey on unsophisticated barrowers. Ultimately those barrowers started defaulting on the bad loans. The media portrayed it in the following way: "The recent economic downturn was the result of banks being forced to make risky loans to African Americans." This was the propaganda repeated daily, mostly on cable media. Cable TV would have you believe that over reaching of poor black folk and Hispanics, with little ability to pay a mortgage, created the financial crisis that almost destroyed the world's banking system.

Nothing could have been father from the truth. The world financial crisis was the outgrowth of greed and opportunity taken by unregulated real estate and financial institutions in the USA.

Some in the media would have you believe that real estate loan defaults made to African Americans created the collapse in the stock market. Nothing could have been father from the truth. The areas with the highest default rates had the smallest black population ie., Miami, Las Vegas, Orlando, Phoenix, and Riverside. These areas do not have high concentrations of African American populations.

The vehicle for the fraud was sub-prime loans and Mortgage Backed Securities. There are two types of cases where someone gets a subprime loan. In the first of the two scenarios, a person who already owns a home wants to refinance the mortgage in order to make significant repairs to the home.

In the second scenario, someone is trying to buy a first home, eager to achieve such a milestone, the buyer neglected to understand the conditions of the loan being offered.

Unscrupulous mortgage brokers and the lending industry preyed on both groups of people. But homeowners and first-time homebuyers with good credit became the victims of predatory lending as well, said Cathy Mickens of Neighborhood Housing Services in Jamaica, Queens.

"It has spread throughout the community," Mickens said, affecting middle-income and high-income people as well as those with lower incomes. Some people who could have gone to a conventional lender and qualified for a standard mortgage will instead go to a predatory lender who promises to

provide the loan quickly and with no documents required. Often, Mickens said, the result is "a disaster."

While some have suggested that borrowers are at fault because of their zeal to own a home, or get-quick money, unscrupulous mortgage brokers, lending institutions and Wall Street investors, motivated by greed and racism, are the driving forces. The result was a financial predatory attack on black wealth.

The second, and most important culprit in this black tragedy was Wall Street. The investor class had concocted a scheme called Mortgage Backed Securities.

The scheme was simple, bundle a group of mortgages and sell them to investors as being safe because the were backed by mortgages. The investment instruments were sold all over the world. When the mortgages started to default the investments started collapsing around the world. African Americans were not the cause of the financial downturn, just the tool. Ultimately the predators were bailed out by governments around the world.

Education—The way to prosperity

Another equalizer in this race to prosperity is a college education. And here the news is good for the black community.

The number of black college students in fall 2012 was 2.3 million, roughly double the number 15 years earlier.

Education does pay off. According to Census statistics, people with a bachelor's degree earn 62 percent more on average than those with only a high school diploma. Over a lifetime, the gap in earning potential between someone with a high school diploma and someone with a bachelor's degree or higher is more than $1 million.

Becoming the new Investor Class

According to the latest survey of black investors by Ariel Capital Management and Charles Schwab, many higher-income African Americans are retreating from the stock market.

After five straight years of steady increases in the percentage of African Americans who own stocks, only 61 percent of blacks surveyed had money in the stock market in 2012, down from 74 percent and approaching the 1998 level of 57 percent. White stock ownership, meanwhile, it is at 79 percent, virtually unchanged over the past six years.

No question black households have to do better, as do many households. But we should cringe when those in our own community talk as if blacks are genetically predisposed to spending on cars and clothes. We have the opportunity to communicate with hundreds of consumers of all ages, race and economic backgrounds, and America—not just black America—is a nation of conspicuous consumers.

Our income is, inch by inch, advancing toward parity with that of our White counterparts. The wealth gap, however, shows no signs of closing. The solution to closing the wealth gap is through a comprehensive financial education program in how they amassed their wealth; thus how we should amass our wealth. We should not make the mistake of getting frustrated about the gap, thereby doing nothing. We should also not make the mistake of following those who would have us believe that those who worked to amass their wealth, (regardless of the means or methods they used to acquire that wealth), should be required to share. We should always understand that we have the capacity, through creativity and dedication, to do the same thing. We don't have to beg anymore.

Bling-Bling Broke

Everything about the way we present ourselves trumpets that we are doing well and living large. A walking billboard of expensive designer labels such as, dresses in $900 St. John Knits and $400 Chanel bags, $200 Ferragamo pumps, and a $50,000 Lexus. But, as the saying goes, "all that glitters is not gold." Our actual net worth—that is, the value of our assets, or what we own, minus the value of our liabilities, or what we owe—is a paltry $20,000, about $50,000 less than someone like a (35 years old with an annual income of $60,000) should be worth. We also carry credit-card debt of nearly $30,000, which amounts to an alarming half of our annual income—and that's not including what we owe on our car. If we were to lose our job, we'd be in big-time trouble.

Too many of us fail to understand that important financial assets are usually the ones we can't see. Unlike stocks, bonds and other financial tools, clothing and furniture, unless they have unique worth as wearable art or collectible antiques, rarely retain their value, much less gain any. (Most financial planners don't even recommend including the value of clothes or personal effects when calculating net worth.)

Many of us now have more money to work with than our foremothers did. In 1996 one in four Black families had incomes of $50,000 or more, and more than 300,000 Black women (one in 26 of the 8.3 million Black female labor force) brought home $50,000 or more. African-American spending tops $400 billion. This kind of money, if deployed strategically, could make African-Americans real players in the world's money markets. We are simply failing to save and invest enough of our hard-won earnings.

As it is, we are such significant players in our nation's consumer markets that entire product lines are shaped around our perceived needs and desires. Our spending patterns clearly show that we are a market worth attracting. According to Target Market News, a leading authority on the Black consumer market, in 1996 we spent $422 million on hosiery; $410 million on CDs, records and tapes; and $339 million on video rentals. In 1995 Black households on average spent 25 percent more than Whites on color televisions. On the other hand, we were 30 percent less likely to save money!

Perhaps such spending indicates how well African-Americans have adapted to the consumer society in which we live. But the fact that social respect comes so hard for Blacks in America may have also made us too vulnerable to consumerist values. Think about it. We spend to establish who we are and to show we have arrived at a certain status, often whether we can afford the display or not. It's as if we feel we can purchase self-esteem by acquiring the trappings of success, so we'll go into debt to do it. But the trappings mean little if creditors are beating down our doors, or if we can't survive three months without a paycheck because we have no savings or investments to cushion us. We don't have to wear our status on our backs. We can take it to the bank! But that would require a shift in our thinking about money, spending and wealth building. It is time that the shifts start to take place. Delay is no longer an option. We have the resource base and the financial capacity, but do we have the will?

Athletes and entertainers earn good money—but they don't even come close to being uber-wealthy, the term Hawkins repeatedly uses without ever defining what he actually means when he says it. 7

Aren't these the stereotypes and false massagers we've spent much of the past 40 years trying to deprogram from American thinking, and black American thinking in particular?

In the age of Obama, why are we still telling each other—and worse, our children—that our best chance to become wealthy in America is through sports and entertainment? Especially when anyone who understands wealth and the American economy, as CNBC and Hawkins surely do, know that is not true?

Ken Fisher's book <u>The Ten Roads to Riches: The Way the Wealthy Got There (And How You Can Too!)</u>, correctly identifies sports and entertainment as the most difficult way to achieve serious wealth, with the longest odds. The primary reasons to pursue a career in sports or entertainment is because you are good at it, and you like to do it—not because you have more than a prayer of ending up with Bob Johnson money.

There are no athletes or entertainers on the most recent <u>Forbes 400 list of the wealthiest Americans</u>. (You needed a net worth of at least $1.3 billion to make the most recent list. Their combined net worth is $1.57 trillion.) It's extremely rare for a recording artist or athlete to maintain his or her earning power past the age of 35.8

To identify the wealthiest black Americans would take a lot of digging—after all, truly wealthy black people, (including many of the corporate CEOs, Wall Street executives and owners of Black Enterprise 100s companies featured in Black Enterprise) are not eager to draw attention to their wealth.

The easy focus on celebrity money, ignorance of the long history of black enterprise and lingering skepticism about the racial loyalties of rich black folks—all combine to obscure the truth about black wealth and business ownership in Southern California.

To most people, black business means mom and pop stores, barbecue stands and barber shops located in the 'hood. These businesses certainly contribute to individual prosperity and neighborhood economies, as well as to local culture. Central Avenue, in its heyday of African American life, represented this kind of vitality. Today, the shops, art galleries, jazz clubs and small merchants located in Leimert Park also offer evidence of a thriving community, in which employment, home ownership and incomes are stable and high.

But the largest black-owned companies aren't to be found in historically black neighborhoods. Instead, they are spread around Los Angeles—in the South Bay, the financial district, in beach communities, downtown and in manufacturing zones. Black entrepreneurs are in high-tech, garment manufacturing, personal services, aluminum processing and distribution, and aerospace. Los Angeles is the only metropolitan area with three sizable black-owned banks; African Americans own and operate construction-equipment suppliers, major auto dealerships, architecture firms, art galleries and insurance and realty firms. L.A. is also home to the "granddaddy" of large black U.S. companies, C.H. James and Son, Inc., established in 1883.

The fact is, more high-income blacks live in Los Angeles County than anywhere else. There are a growing number of them who own businesses and assets that comprise real wealth. The most recent Census figures show that there are 32,645 black-owned businesses in the county, with total revenue of more that $3.6 billion and 25,082 employees.

These companies are run by African American entrepreneurs who not only successfully compete in the open market and create wealth, but also give back to their communities. The range of their community, civic and charitable involvement is wide. According to Patricia Means, publisher of Turning Point magazine and a member of the board of the Jenessee Center shelter for battered women and children, these entrepreneurs exhibit "a commitment to not only do good for [themselves], but to do good for the community. It comes from tradition. We have been taught to reach back and help somebody. You're not successful if you don't."

They are living proof that Frazier's generalizations about the black bourgeoisie are outdated.

Compared with other companies, a study by the Joint Center for Political and Economic Studies shows, black businesses "were more likely to participate in programs to assist young people, welfare recipients and *individuals from high-poverty neighborhoods." Indeed, a distinguishing mark of many black-owned companies is a dedication to diversity in their work forces. For example, out of 40 employees at Bazile Metals Service, with annual sales of $15 million, 60% are African American, 35% Latino and 5% white. President Barry Bazile also operates Welfare to Work Partners, a nonprofit that provides education, training and jobs for low-income participants.*

Many blacks were first-time owners in their industry and are eager to find ways to keep the doors open for those who follow them. Carl Burhanan, owner of Oasis Aviation, aspires to grow his Marina del Rey-based fuel-supply business from current sales of $41.3 million to $100 million. Yet, aware of his own experiences of racism inside and outside the military, Burhanan helped found the 300-member U.S. Army Black Aviation Assn., which gives scholarships to African American students who want to pursue an aviation career.

Education is a high priority for socially conscious black entrepreneurs. Clarissa Faye Howard, owner of Bd Systems, offers internships for inner-city youth at her $40-million-a-year firm. The founder of the $80-million Act 1 Personnel Services, Janice Bryant Howroyd, funds scholarships for students attending historically black colleges, company internships and, in conjunction with The Links, an exclusive black women's club, works on a mentoring program, Project Life, for low-income youths in Carson schools. Eric Hanks, who grosses $1 million in annual sales as owner of M. Hanks Gallery, teaches affordable classes on art appreciation and speaks regularly at public schools. Karl Kani, whose company employs 45 and takes in $69 million in annual sales, serves on the advisory board of the Mayor's after-school enrichment program, L.A.'s Best.

Black businesses' emphasis on "giving back" flows from fresh memories of discrimination and the knowledge that the history of race in America is in part one of the economic subordination of black people, beginning with slavery and continuing, after Reconstruction, with the exclusion of blacks *from certain occupations and professions. Black business owners like Henry O'Bryant, who began in the 1950s by manufacturing uniforms for once-fledgling companies like McDonald's, recalls being told at the Frank Wiggins Trade School that tailoring classes were "reserved for white kids." Broadway Federal Bank, with $139.5 million in assets and $119 million in deposits, was established in 1946 by H. Claude Hudson, dentist and Los Angeles NAACP founder, to satisfy the post-World War II demand for homeownership when black GIs were denied mortgages by mainstream banks.*

L.A.'s black business owners, however, tend not to harbor anger over the inequities of the past or present. They are more likely to exhibit the faith of Biddy Mason. Mason, a former slave, built a fortune in downtown real estate and nursing homes before her death in 1891. In addition to her business acumen, she founded a church and was a philanthropist and political agitator. Mason taught that, "If you hold your hand closed, nothing good can come in. The open hand is blessed, for it gives in abundance, even as it receives."

Political debate among blacks still makes much of the contentious rift between Booker T. Washington and W.E.B. Du Bois over which road leads to freedom. Du Bois, a founder of the National Assn. for the Advancement of Colored People, criticized Washington, president of Tuskegee Institute, for embracing black capitalism and shying away from what he considered to be necessary political engagement on behalf of full rights for all blacks. What few know is that the idea for Washington's premiere organization, the National Negro Business League, founded in 1900, came from Du Bois. It was Du Bois who organized the university conference at which he proposed the federation of local businesses that would enable black people to join "the industrial and mercantile spirit of the age."

If generating economic power means stronger black representation in society and politics, there is obviously scant cause for scoffing at black wealth. African American entrepreneurs face the same challenges as other business owners, and then some. They battle traces of historical discrimination, a lack of available capital and the tough competition that marks the huge, diverse L.A. market, the biggest business base in the country. Here, where the African American population has always been proportionately low, black-owned businesses are vastly outnumbered not only by those owned by whites, but also by those run by Latinos and Asian Americans.

Given history's shameful determination to limit black economic independence, African American entrepreneurs have a unique story to share about the arc of success. But their real success lies in a near-universal commitment to community and civic service. Theirs is a corporate model worth emulating.

Oprah Winfrey tops the inaugural Forbes list of the Wealthiest Black American. Oprah Winfrey is one of the most lucrative brands in the world. Today the Oprah Winfrey Show airs in 144 countries, drawing 44 million U.S. viewers each week. Her Harpo Productions helped create the likes of Dr. Phil and Rachael Ray. She's produced Broadway shows and has her own satellite radio channel. For all of this, she consistently earns more than $200 million a year.

And unlike many others on our list, her business is weathering the recession well. Winfrey continues to entice viewers with money-saving tips, celebrity interviews and relationship advice. She launched a new show this past fall, which will be hosted by frequent guest Dr. Oz, and is planning to launch The Oprah Winfrey Network early next year.

With a net worth of $2.7 billion, Winfrey tops the inaugural Forbes list of the Wealthiest Black Americans. She is the only billionaire on the list of 20 tycoons, all of whom are self-made. The group built their fortunes across a spectrum of industries spanning athletics and entertainment, media, investments, real estate, construction and restaurants.

Black Entertainment Television founder Robert Johnson became the first African American billionaire in 2000 after he sold the network to Viacom

(VIA—news—people) for $3 billion in stock and assumed debt. Since then, sagging Viacom and CBS (CBS—news—people) stock, plus investments in real estate, hotels and banks—industries pummeled in the past year amid the recession—have dragged Johnson's net worth to $550 million, we estimate. He ranks third on the list; his former wife and BET co-founder, Sheila Johnson, ranks seventh with $400 million.

Wealthiest African-Americans

The following list is the ranking of America's richest Black Americans on May 6, 2009.

Wealthiest African-Americans

#	Name	Net worth (USD)	Residence	Sources of wealth
1	Oprah Winfrey	$2.7 billion	Illinois	Harpo Productions
2	Tiger Woods	$600 million	Florida	Golf, endorsements
3	Robert Johnson	$550 million	Florida	BET, hotel investments
4	Michael Jordan	$525 million	Illinois	Basketball, Nike, endorsements
5	Earvin "Magic" Johnson, Jr.	$500 million	California	Basketball, real estate, investments
6	William Henry Cosby, Jr.	$450 million	Massachusetts	The Cosby Show, entertainment
7	Sheila Johnson	$400 million	Virginia	BET, investments
8	R. Donahue Peebles	$350 million	Florida	Real estate
9	Berry Gordy, Jr.	$325 million	California	Motown Records, Jobete Records
10	Quintin Primo III	$300 million	Illinois	Real estate

11	Don King	$290 million	Florida	Boxing, Promotions
12	Janice Bryant Howroyd & family	$250 million	California	Staffing, Investments
13	Herman J. Russell	$200 million	Georgia (U.S. state)	Construction, real estate
14	Ulysses Bridgeman, Jr.	$200 million	Georgia (U.S. state)	Restaurants
15	Tracy Maitland	$150 million	Kentucky	Investments
16	Alphonse Fletcher, Jr.	$150 million	New York	Investments
17	Shawn "Jay-Z" Carter	$150 million	New York	Rocawear, Entertainment, investments
18	Kobe Bryant	$140 million	California	Basketball, endorsements
19	Shaquille O'Neal	$130 million	Arizona	Basketball, endorsements
20	Kenneth I. Chenault	$125 million	New York	American Express

Top 5 African American CEOs

The Africans Americans in the United States have really carved a niche for themselves in the corporate world. There are over 75 black men and women in the list of the highest-ranking executives, of which 8 are Chief Executive Officers (CEOs). Only eight black executives have ever made it to the Chairman or CEO position of a "Fortune 500" listed company. The "Fortune 500" is a list of the 500 largest companies in the United States.

1. Kenneth Chenault has been the CEO of AMEX (American Express) since 2001.

2. *Ronald A. Williams*
   Aetna, a major health insurance firm, is run by.

3. *Ursula Burns is the first female African-American CEO of an S&P 100. She serve as chairwoman and CEO of Xerox. She is the first African-American woman CEO to head a Fortune 500 company. In 2009, Forbes ranked her the 14th most powerful woman in the world.*

4. *Clarence Otis, Jr.*
   Runs Darden Restaurants, an org. with 18,000+ franchises.

5. *Ephren W. Taylor II*
   Taylor, 29 year old is not only the youngest African American CEO but also the youngest American CEO ever. He was named as the CEO of City Capital Corporation in 2006. the CEO but also a philanthropist, author, inspirational speaker and a national T.V host.

Blacks are economically depressed

Another common misperception of African-Americans is that on the whole, blacks are economically depressed or poor in the United States. Once again, media crime reports from the 'ghetto,' hip-hop videos and gangsta rap do not show an accurate picture of black American wealth as a whole.

There is a projection that based on purchasing power alone, African-Americans eclipse all African countries and many emerging countries. African-American purchasing power is projected to exceed $1 trillion by 2012. This figure outstrips most other countries GDP. In fact, if African Americans were a country, it would be the tenth largest economy in the world today.9

The numerous portrayals in the mainstream media of black poverty and the seemingly "permanent" underclass do not reflect the overall wealth of African-Americans in the USA.

If the African-American portion of the US GDP was separated from the rest of the US GDP, its $688 Billion would still eclipse most Third World and indeed many other "developed" countries, including Sweden.10

Not too many countries can match this amount, and blacks only have 13% of the US population. Many other countries make do with less GDP, and with many more people. The true test for the future is the effective use of this massive wealth to achieve proper respect.

6

MAKE YOUR VOTE COUNT

THE NEW POLITICS IN AMERICA . . .
THE AWAKENING

The recent election of President Barack Obama signaled an awakening for African Americans in United States. Until the recent election, the African American voting population, was ignored by republicans and courted only in a close election by Democrats. This was a tactic designed by politicians to control the vote of African Americans while minimizing their influence or rewards after an election. The recent threat of a Blackout (African Americans refusing to vote en mass) in the general election sent shockwaves throughout the Democratic Party before the presidential election of 2008.

The election of Barack Obama was significant to African American pride, but far more important was the message; the Democrats cannot elect a president without the African American vote.

From this day forward, African Americans should understand the value and power of our vote. We must have a well thought out agenda to improve our lives through our vote. African Americans now know that they have true political value; the challenge is to use it wisely; forty years of wandering in the political wilderness was required to get to come to this realization. Political Analyst, Pat Buchanan, has predicted black complacency in the 2010/2012 elections.

During the early presidential campaign, Obama was never really considered a viable candidate, by neither White America, nor Black America. Most of White America was not yet ready for a black president, and Black Americans dared not dream. Whites scoffed and Blacks, who were reluctant, supported Hillary Clinton.

I was surprised at the media's of depiction of Obama's campaign; which was portrayed as Barack and Michelle sitting around a dirty kitchen table, counting twenty dollar donations from poor black people. The media perpetuated the perception that this campaign was managed by the local civic association. Nothing could have been further from the truth.

After Obama's victory in Iowa, some African Americans dared to dream, while others continued to support Hillary Clinton. The media ravaged Hillary after Iowa; creating a white backlash vote in New Hampshire. It was the New Hampshire win and the subsequent "Jessie Jackson" statement by Bill Clinton after Obama's victory in South Carolina that created the black awakening. African Americans accounted for the majority of Democratic voters in South Carolina, with 55 percent—the highest turnout among African-Americans in any Democratic Presidential Primary for which data is available. A huge proportion of them, 78 percent, supported Obama; compared to 19 percent for Hillary Clinton and just 2 percent for John Edwards.

After the South Carolina win by Obama, and Bill Clinton's "Jessie Jackson" reference; CNN's Dona Brazil expressed her outrage and coined the term "Blackout", meaning that in November African Americans would stay away from the polls, if the election was unfairly stolen from Obama. The Democratic Party knew that would doom any chance of electing any other Democrat as president.

Something emerged after the South Carolina primary and they began to realize that the Obama campaign was more than existent; it was history in the making It was superbly financed but also tactical and strategic in its thinking and planning. In an article by Robert Schlesinger, it was pointed out how important the Black vote was in the primaries, but wasn't quite sure about the general election[2] I think that some knew that they would have a tremendous effect on the general election, based on the demographics of the Electoral College. The black demographic proved to be critical in the Obama general election strategy, just as some analysts knew, and that the old strategy was no longer valid.

Electoral College votes won the presidency. There were many states that had large concentrations of African American populations who will forever affect the Electoral College. The following article proves the point.

Do Democrats Need the Black Vote?
By Robert Schlesinger

"How much do black voters matter to Democrats in a presidential election? Try 76 electoral votes worth.

The aforementioned statistics should validate the value of black voters for national elections in the future. Complacency is no longer an option for black voters. Don't repeat the lesson of the post Jessie Jackson presidential run in the 80's, in which frustration over Jessie's unsuccessful run caused an opting out of

*the political process. This ultimately caused the black vote to be
rendered valueless except in close races.*

*The recent 85% turnout established the true power of the black
electorate."*

*"Here's the deal on politics and race in America: Republicans
don't need black voters, but they want them. Democrats don't
want black voters, but they need them. Blacks have been the
Democrats' most loyal voters since the 1960s, typically giving
the party upward of 90% of their vote. But Democrats ignore
blacks."*

*That's according to none other than the Rev. Jesse Jackson, who
said precisely that. "The black vote will remain captive to the
Democrat Party as long as black people see themselves as victims
and view the Democrats as the party of 'civil rights'."*

The relationship between African Americans and the Democrats
can be comparable to that of a john and an unpaid prostitute. Most
black Americans have been Democrats since the 1960s. What have
the Democrats done for us in all that time? We have the lowest
average income of any large racial group in the nation. We're
incarcerated at an alarmingly high rate. We are still segregated and
profiled, and have a very low representation at the top echelons of
the Democratic Party. We are the stalwarts, the bulwark, the Old
Faithful of the Democrats, and yet they have not made our issues a
high priority in a very long time. If we had our own political voting
bloc, that paid attention to issues that reflect our needs in domestic
and international affairs, things would change for us. For starters,
many more African Americans would be likely to vote. Imagine the
interest young people would have if they felt we were organizing
based on our own interests. They could work for a candidate who
represented their issues or they could even run for office themselves.

If we took the vote into our own hands, we would not have to ask the Democrats for their support—we could demand it. Imagine it. We could actually democratize America by taking power away from the two-party system and handing it over to the people. Other special parties would arise, splintering off from the centrist attendants of the rich, once we show them the way.

What I'm talking about here is the beginning of an American Evolution; a movement that will create a series of political interest groups that will transform our two-party system into a virtual parliament, where we are able to construct smaller political groups based on specific interests. There could be Black Party Congress members from Watts, Harlem, the Motor City and a dozen other inner-city defenders. All we have to do is have a fair representation in the House of Representatives to have an extraordinary impact on the wheels of government.

It is past the time when we African Americans can complain about how we are treated without trying to take the reins of power for ourselves. A Black Voting Bloc would be a bold move. Some might say a radical move—too radical. If we could come together and see a way to put balance back in the American political landscape, then we should do it. Why? . . . Because if we do not lead, then we will be led. And if those who have learned to despise, distrust and diminish us are the leaders, then our path will lead us even further away from our original homes. We will wake up like strangers in our own beds. We, and our children, will be walking in uncomfortable shoes to poor jobs. We will be jeered on every corner, and every mirror we come across will distort our image.

Just so that it doesn't seem that I'm giving a short explanation to this argument, let me try to explain why this kind of "political party" will be different from its interest-corporation counterparts. First, this kind of group will be a political unit more than a party. This unit should be patterned after interest groups that form around specific necessities of our particular community. As I've mentioned before, I would like to see many of these units evolve, but for the moment let me address the Black Voting Bloc.

What we need for this group is a short list of demands that define our political aspirations at any given point. These demands might change over time, but at any given moment we should have no more than eight expectations of the candidates or legislators we vote for. I am not positioning myself as the leader, or even as a central designer of this group, but let me put forward a list of possible demands that our unit might embrace.

All African Americans do not have to join right away. If we can assemble 10 percent of the black voting population, we can wield a great deal of power. Others will join us if our political strategy works. In time, we might tip the scales against the rich and the super wealthy. If we are able to tip the scales, we might very well be able to make this a better world.

I know many of you will say that we do not have the time to allow the United States to evolve politically. Like many Americans, you believe that our nation faces urgent problems that must be solved by the next election and the elections after that. My answer is not to think what they want you to think. Our so-called political parties want you to believe that only they can save you when, really, they have no intention of doing so. Both the Democrats and the Republicans are in business for themselves, in this vast religion of capitalism. They will never solve America's problems; not fully. We have to strive against the system, change it, and make it reflect our inexpert visions of right and good. As long as you vote Democratic, as long as you vote Republican, you will be assuring that true democracy has no chance to exist. As long as we believe in the fear mongers' light show, the world will suffer under our misguided convictions.

There is no question that a Black Voting Bloc would be a fine context for us and for people of the Black Diasporas around the world. It would be a forum that would express perceptions from the underbelly of the American experience. That experience, I believe, would find resonance on an international scale and help to bring our maverick nation into concert with certain other countries that would like to co-exist with us harmoniously.

But how do we get black people to feel strongly about political unity? What in our experience will bring us together? Should we turn to a charismatic leader to guide us safely through the minefield of fanaticism? I have been told so many times that the problem in this world is that so-and-so died too young. A couple of years ago I heard another public figure say that it was because Robert Kennedy died that American liberalism lost its way. What might Martin Luther King Jr. or Malcolm X have achieved if assassins' bullets had not cut them down in their prime?

If only we had leaders now like we did back then, so many lament. It's hard for me to write these words without a hint of sarcasm. Nostalgia belongs in the retirement home. Any organization, movement or people who rely solely (or even greatly) on a charismatic leader for their strength and their motivation are in the most precarious position possible.

"Cut off the head and the body will fall," their enemies murmur. This is a way to let those enemies dissolve your context. Just put all your belief in one leader, and sooner or later you will be lost.

Some might say that I should end this section with those words. This may be true, but I think they open the door to other considerations.

We do need leadership. We have to have people who will make decisions and blaze trails; people who will stand up to warmongers and moneylenders; people who might create context, illuminate the darkness with an electronic billboard; people who could organize our vote.

I could spend a lot of time and space here criticizing our current leaders, but what would be the purpose? No matter how much they have lost their way, these leaders are not our enemies. If I follow a man or woman who is leading me astray, then I have to accept my own culpability and blindness.

Someone in a later year may ask, "Didn't you see the millions dying in Africa while your leaders argued about the references and jokes in the movie Barbershop?" And how will we answer? If we don't lie, we might say, "I knew what was happening, but I didn't know how to act. I felt powerless and helpless and so I did nothing."

The truth hurts. We all know that. But if we can see that we need leadership and that we don't have the leadership we need, then we might begin to question why. I believe a vacuum in our leadership has been caused by a natural conservatism in the black community that echoes the smug confidence of America in general. This conservatism harbors a deep dread of our young people.

America has carried the notion of property and power to such an intensely negative degree that we have very little room left for humanity and art in our hearts. We work long hours, eat bad food, close our eyes to the atrocities committed in our name and spend almost everything we make on the drugs that keep us from succumbing to the emptiness of our spiritual lives. We gobble down antidepressants, sleeping pills, martinis, sitcoms and pornography in a desperate attempt to keep balance in this soul-less limbo.

In a world where poetry is a contest at best and a competition at worst; where the importance of a painting is gauged by the price it can be sold for—we are to be counted among the lost. And so when I say that we need leaders and that those leaders must come from our youth, it is no idle statement. We need our young people because without their dreams to guide us we will have only cable TV and grain alcohol for succor.

Oh, how I wish the above statements were mine. The fact is that they were the thoughts of Ramesh Ponnuru and Richard Nadler published in the National Review, March 5, 2001. The message was too important, in my view, to not publish it again in this text.

Why aren't Republicans doing better? In the past, they neglected black areas deliberately, for tactical reasons. They understood that blacks were not as liberal as they were Democratic, and that there are black conservatives who oppose abortion, gun control, and high taxes, just like their white counterparts. But they calculated that a campaign to increase the Republican share of the black vote would backfire if it also increased black turnout. That strategy, whatever its morality, made pragmatic sense when black turnout was low, but it cannot work when black turnout is high. Democrats have been able to stimulate record black turnout in selected media markets. They have done so both by hyping imaginary racial crises and by blaming Republicans for real problems.

Until we start to understand that to share in the wealth in this country, we must influence the politics. When we allow our tremendous political influence to be so marginalized, we become what we are today, beggars. We have the power to influence the outcome of any election in the country. How did we allow ourselves to be lead to believe that we were so impudent, that we had to depend on the generosity of others? We changed the political landscape in this country in the last presidential election. We functioned as a group, led not by a leader, but by an agenda—our agenda. We can begin to solve most of our problems in one election cycle; if we were to readjust our mindset from being led to leading. In the future, no one should ever emerge as our leader, since they have the ability to be co-opted by the system. We should set and control our agenda. We should demand that our selected representatives, represent ONLY our views. We can and we must lead ourselves.

7

MEDIA STEREOTYPE
THE MEDIA NIGGAS

Media Matter

*P*erceptions are formed by what you see and hear. The perceptions of African Americans are shaped by the media locally, nationally, and internationally. Occasionally, ratings are the driving force in what is aired; therefore the media portrays African Americans as ignorant, lazy, irresponsible, welfare grubbing, drug infected, and dangerous. In most instances we are robbing, selling drugs, or raping. It is not unusual for foreign visitors to feel threatened in the presence of black people.

Black staffs in hotels are constantly reminded by foreign guest that they are uncomfortable in their presence because of how they are portrayed in the media. It is not unusual for a guest at hotels to call for service at night, yet they refused to open the door if they see a black staff person. They usually request that you return in the morning when they feel safer.

Most media representation of black kids is that they are slow learners, discipline problems, and mostly products of single parent, struggling homes.

The really sad thing is that the more kids see this image of them the more they tend to believe it.

Negative propaganda is insidious, in most news pieces that are about unemployment, the featured character is usually black. If the issue is positive and uplifting, the featured character is white. In news articles about drug abuse, if the outcome is negative, the character is always black. Take the same story featuring a white character, the person is in successful rehab, and now enrolled at Harvard.

When this type of propaganda is constantly shown, it is only reasonable to conclude that, blacks always fail, and whites will always succeed.

The media cannot be held totally responsible; we have those among us who will not pass up any opportunity to be who will feed into that narrative. They will sell out their culture and themselves just to be noticed. Turn on the camera and lights and some black folk will act like newly freed slaves. They will denigrate themselves and their race. This only perpetuates the image of no dignity or self respect. Professional athletes are sometimes the worse offenders. However, I am always proud when I watch LeBron James, of the Miami Heat basketball team, every interview is thoughtful, articulate, and informative. He is more representative of the new athlete.

About five or six years ago, radio talk show host, Don Imus took the liberty of referring to a mostly black women's college basketball team as a bunch of "NAPPI HEADED HO'S". Imus's reputation was as a loose tongue, say anything morning radio host, with millions of loyal fans. His list of sponsors was impressive. His earnings were in the millions of dollars. His friends were among the most powerful in the business sector, and government. Yet when he made that statement on that morning, his sponsor support immediately dried up. What followed only served to validate my long held position that, America is about the almighty dollar, and it will not allow anyone or anything to influence that.

This incident should have served as an awakening for black folk, because what followed was most enlightening. From this insult came corporate America's response to the threat to their almighty dollar.

Don Imus had insulted a population that had a GDP value of almost a TRILLION DOLLARS. A large part is used to purchase products that sponsor the Don Imus Show. Corporate America had to make a decision about what African American's response would be about the insult, and how they would feel about those who would sponsor it. Black folk could abandon their products. ONE TRILLION DOLLARS in buying power was about to abandon their brands. Corporate America made a swift and decisive decision, DROP IMUS NOW.

African Americans should have come away from that experience with an understanding that ONE TRILLION DOLLARS in spending power is louder than ten Million Man Marches.

Your value, your dignity is in the volume of your money. Your protest should no longer be protest marches; it should be the threat of withholding your money. Your power is your money. African Americans should understand that; if they were a separate country, it would be the twenty third riches country in the world. We don't have to accept commercial abuse any longer.

The Imus story was not to relate an insult in the media. The real purpose of the Imus story was to encourage black Americans to never allow themselves to be victims again. When the media chose to take liberties with our dignity, don't complain to the media, complain to the sponsors. With ONE TRILLION in your wallet you should never feel like a victim again.

From this day forward, we should warn the media that you can not portray black Americans in that insulting way again.

African Americans have always allowed the media to define who we are.

If you have watched, listened to, and read American media all of your life, you probably have filed these images into your thinking process: African-Americans are mostly athletes, rap stars, drug addicts, welfare mothers, criminals, and/or murderers. Latinos are illegal aliens, ignorant immigrants who take, but gives little back to the country and can barely speak the language or drug-crazed thugs who have no respect for law or order. Asian-Americans are weak, model citizens or inscrutable, manipulative, uncaring invaders of business—especially in the United States. Native Americans are illiterate, drunken Indians who hate all Caucasians and sleep away their lives.

If you are like most middle-class Americans, most of what you know about members of other races or religions comes from what you read in the paper, hear on the radio, or see on television. When you ignore all of the self-righteous posturing of the media, it is easy to see that racial and ethnic stereotypes still dominate much of reporting today.

A good deal of the problem has to do with the definition of what is news. If much of today's TV news, for example, is defined as crime stories, a number of the pieces presented may seem derogatory toward people of minority racial and ethnic backgrounds because many of the crimes are committed by poor people with little to lose, and many poor people are members of racial and ethnic minorities. Since all viewers and readers get is a steady stream of minority-dominated crime, the impression left is clear: Racial and ethnic minorities, in the descriptive phrase of the president of the National Association of Black Journalists, "usually have criminal faces."

African-Americans Are Held to a Different and Higher Standard

It didn't take long to notice the media's uneven portrayal of Black and White behavior in Katrina's aftermath. The White family wading in waist-deep water was "foraging" for food in order to survive. But the Black family, under identical circumstances, came upon their goods by "stealing" and "looting."

The One Who Labels Possesses the Power

The labels, "victims of Katrina" and "evacuees" surfaced quickly in the news. But most disturbing for me was the "refugee" label associated with this group. The sight of masses of people languishing on makeshift cots, combined with the term "refugee," allowed us to subconsciously shift the setting of this tragedy to some "other group of people" in some distant land. Was the media providing subtle cues to the American public in order to make this disaster, and those who were experiencing it, seem foreign and removed from our spheres of existence? These labels immediately suggest that these individuals' abilities are sub par.

KATRINA & MEDIA MYTH-MAKING: FRAMING THE POOR

During the flooding of New Orleans in the wake of Hurricane Katrina, many a voice praised the media for its supposedly aggressive coverage. The fact that Anderson Cooper cried on camera, or that Geraldo evinced outrage (imagine that), or that even Fox's Shepard Smith waxed indignant at the suffering in the streets, was taken as evidence of some newfound courage on the part of the press.

But just as surely as the media went after those in positions of power, and sought to expose them as witless in all respects, it was even more adept at framing (pun very much intended) low-income black folks in the streets of New Orleans as a collection of deviant criminals. In other words, the more things changed, the more they ultimately stayed the same, especially with the press presenting images of the desperate and left behind that reinforced negative and racist stereotypes, to the utter exclusion of accuracy and fair-mindedness.

An example of reinforced negativism was the constant repetition of the same five or six video loops of so-called looters. The fact that most of these people were taking water, food and medicine, didn't seem to matter to camerapersons or, ultimately, a viewing public quick to condemn what they saw. Never mind that the relative paucity of such video suggesting theft wasn't particularly representative of the crowds on Canal Street—after all, if looting had been that common, there would have been more than the same half-dozen clips to present. This appears not to matter as well.

An even better case in point is the repetition of unfounded rumors—later proven false—to the effect that Children's Hospital had been raided by drug addicts looking for a fix; or that gang rapes were occurring in the Superdome or Convention Center, or that babies were being molested and then having their throats slit, only to be stuffed like trash in abandoned freezers and garbage cans. False, false and false; and for none of these stories had there ever been a first hand witness who had actually seen any of the supposed carnage taking place.

Yet the media, feeling no need to find witnesses or to verify claims of black deviance (because, after all, what's not to believe?) simply went along. The result? Rescue efforts were delayed because rescue workers had been scared for their lives by a press that led them to think New Orleans was a war zone; the Governor and Mayor actually told law enforcement to stop saving lives and start arresting and shooting lawbreakers on sight; and the public, which rarely needs reasons to think the worst of poor black people, found its stereotypes confirmed. Not only whites, it should be pointed out, but black folks too, like Mayor Nagin and his crony police chief

Eddie Compass, both of whom apparently think so little of their own people that they too assumed the stories were true, in spite of no evidence, and repeated the charges on national TV.

First, there was the one about the crack dealer who refused to be evacuated to a hospital because he wouldn't be able to sell his wares there; then there was the one about the thugs (black and poor of course) who destroyed a rest area on the Louisiana/Texas border, during a stop on the way to Houston, even urinating on the walls to show their disregard for civilized norms of behavior; then there was the one from the guy claiming to have volunteered at the Astrodome to feed and help evacuees, all to be shocked by how ungrateful they were—supposedly demanding beer, liquor, cigarettes and four-star restaurant meals. That hundreds of others refuted these nonsensical claims, and noted how unbelievably gracious the evacuees had been, did nothing to damper the enthusiasm with which the lies were circulated.

Though the mainstream media hadn't created these phony and vicious stories (and indeed, one has to wonder what kind of evil mind and heart would have done so), it is certainly true that they created the conditions that made such tripe believable to a lot of people. Had the media focused less on looters and supposed gang raping murderers, and more on the efforts by thousands to help one another in the midst of hellish conditions—stories that are only trickling out in the corporate press, but which those who lived through them have been trying to get told via their own accounts from the flood zone—it would have been impossible for such vile trash as this to have gained traction. But once the climate had been created and the frame set—one that said, these are bad people, who do bad things—it took no effort at all for racists to concoct lies and peddle those to a willing and gullible public that never seems to challenge stories of black perfidy. Instead, they so easily fit within their pre-existing racist biases in the first place.

Which brings us to the other big lie told about the poor in New Orleans and has yet to be addressed in the media, despite how easily it can be disproved by a mere five minutes worth of research. Namely, it is the argument that the reason 130,000 poor black folks were unable to escape the flooding was because they had grown dependent on the government to save them, thanks to the "welfare state," and that was why they lacked the money and cars to get out before disaster struck.

In other words, liberal social policy had rendered the black poor unable or unwilling to work, content to collect a government check, and thus, had made them incapable of saving themselves.

To begin with, as of 2004, according to the Census Bureau, there were only 4600 households in all of New Orleans receiving cash welfare from the nation's principal aid program, TANF (Temporary Assistance for Needy Families, formerly Aid to Families With Dependent Children, or AFDC). That is not a misprint: 4600 out of a total of 130,000 households in the black community alone. Which means that even if every welfare receiving household in Orleans Parish had been black (which was not in fact the case), this would have represented only a little more than four percent of black households in the city.

According to the same Census data, the average household size in a welfare receiving family in New Orleans is the same as the citywide average for non-recipients: roughly 3.5 persons. So the number of individuals receiving welfare in New Orleans, by the time of Katrina would have been about 16,000.

Thus, even if we assume that all of the 130,000 persons left behind were poor, and that no persons receiving welfare managed to escape before the flooding with friends or family, this would mean that at most, perhaps twelve percent of the persons left behind (and whose faces we may have been seeing on national TV) would not have been welfare recipients at all, let alone persons who had been rendered dependent on such benefits for long periods of time.

And speaking of dependence, or the notion that the city's welfare recipients had grown content to sit back and collect government checks instead of doing for self, this hardly seems likely when you consider that the average annual income received from TANF, for those small numbers actually getting any such benefits at all, was only a little more than $2,800 per year, in New Orleans prior to the catastrophe.

Indeed, such paltry amounts explain why most of the poor in New Orleans, far from being happy to receive so-called handouts, work whenever they can find steady employment, which admittedly, is not often the case.

For example, in the ninety-eight percent black and forty percent poor Lower Ninth Ward, one of the hardest hit communities (and one about which many negative things were said in terms of so-called welfare dependence), seventy-one percent of families prior to the flooding reported income from paid employment, while only eight percent received income from cash welfare. In other words, folks in this community were almost nine times more likely to earn their pay than to receive government benefits. Forty percent of workers from the community worked full-time, and the average commute time for Ninth Ward workers was over 45 minutes each day, suggesting that the work ethic was quite common to the folks who lived there, irrespective of commonly held and utterly false stereotypes.

Even food stamps—a program with much more lenient terms and where even the near poor can often qualify for minimal benefits—were only received by eleven percent of New Orleans households as of last year: hardly indicative of a general mindset of welfare entitlement. As for public housing, far from being the location of residence for most poor blacks in New Orleans—let alone those in the streets in the wake of Katrina—fewer than 20,000 people lived in such units at the time of the flooding: this representing no more than five percent of black New Orleanians. In the Lower Ninth Ward, for example, few lived in public housing and nearly six in ten families owned their own homes.

Even in the city's poorest communities, like the Iberville or Lafitte housing developments, or parts of Central City, at least a third, and often a majority of households report income from paid employment. What's more, tenants in the B.W. Cooper development have been managing their own housing for years, teaching job and leadership skills to the persons who live there.

Likewise, in the mid-90s, several public housing developments participated in a national Jobs Program, funded by the Annie B. Casey Foundation: a successful effort that matched low-income black residents with businesses looking for employees. In the former St. Thomas development—the first public housing "project" funded by the federal government under the Roosevelt Administration—residents had started their own coffee shop and bookstore, and had created innovative teen pregnancy prevention and safe sex initiatives.

Bottom line: the stereotype of poor blacks in New Orleans (and elsewhere) as lazy and dependent on government is false. In Louisiana, it should be noted that only a very small share of those receiving TANF benefits, and AFDC before that, are able-bodied adults. Indeed, even prior to welfare reform, only eleven percent of those receiving AFDC in the state were able-bodied adults who did no work: the rest were vulnerable children, the elderly, the disabled, or adults who were already working (mostly part-time), but earned too little to come off assistance.

It should also be noted that even when persons do receive so-called welfare, there is still a predicate to doing so: one that is rarely explored, but is simply assumed to be personal incompetence, bad choice-making, laziness or other personal pathologies. So, for example, we are to believe that for those who live in public housing, it was their own lack of initiative or willingness to take personal responsibility for their lives that rendered them so vulnerable to the likes of Hurricane Katrina and the collapse of the city's levees.

Yet what this commonly-repeated claim ignores is what came before folks ended up in public housing, in overcrowded communities, with concentrated levels of extreme poverty; and what came before had nothing to do with the welfare state, or liberal social policy more generally. Rather, what happened was the deliberate and calculated destruction of the inner-city in the name of economic "development" (which benefited only the elite) and to meet the needs of middle-class and above whites.

So, for example, consider the Treme (pronounced truh-may): the oldest free black neighborhood in the United States, home to Congo Square and Louis Armstrong Park. Located on the outer edge of the French Quarter and Central Business District, the Treme is more than ninety percent black and over half of its residents are poor, when you include those in the Iberville and Lafitte housing developments. Though it had long been a lower-income community, with the attendant issues that often emerge in such spaces, the Treme had also been, for the most part, functional. It was the site of dozens of successful black-owned businesses, and hundreds of stable middle-class families, where few lived in the so-called projects. The same was true for the 7th Ward: the base of the city's old-line Creole community.

But beginning in the early 1960s, the city of New Orleans, as with every major city in the United States, began taking federal funds to extend interstate highways through their urban centers, which meant the heart of those black communities. In New Orleans, plans to extend the interstate through the French Quarter met with stiff opposition from affluent (and mostly white) historic preservationists and business owners. Once their political clout was deployed so as to block construction through the main tourist artery, planners opted to take the I-10 through the Treme and 7th Ward, whose lower income and black residents lacked the power to stop their property from being destroyed in the name of progress.

It was a story repeated throughout the U.S. during this time. By the mid-1960s, interstate construction in urban areas was destroying roughly 37,000 residences annually. This, in addition to the 40,000 more that were being torn down each year in the name of "urban renewal," which translated into the building of shopping malls, office parks and parking lots. By 1969, nearly 70,000 homes, mostly occupied by blacks and Latinos, were being destroyed for the interstate program alone, in virtually every medium and large city in the country.

Although some had argued for financial assistance to help relocate the low-income families displaced by this process, rarely did such help materialize. Indeed, less than ten percent of those displaced by urban renewal had new single-resident occupancy housing to go to afterward. Instead, they had to double up with relatives in small, crowded apartments, or move into public housing projects, which became something akin to concentration camps for the poorest and most vulnerable citizens of the nation.

These policies, known euphemistically as "slum clearance" by those who implemented and supported them, actually created slums, in places which previously had been low-income, but largely working class and stable communities. In New Orleans, this also extended to the Central Business District, including the very land where the now infamous Superdome sits.

Beginning in 1971, construction began on the facility, on which ground had previously existed, yet another mostly black and largely low-income and working class neighborhood. But in a contest between the needs and lives of those New Orleanians on the one hand, and the mere wants of wealthy developers, concert promoters, the New Orleans Saints and Tulane University boosters on the other (the latter of which wanted to move their pathetic team's games there, away from the old and decrepit Sugar Bowl), which side can we guess, ultimately prevailed? And so the Dome was completed, in 1975, at a public cost of tens of millions of dollars, and the loss of yet another patch of homesteads for the city's black majority.

All of this "slum clearance," it should be noted, was done for the benefit of whites, and not only the rich developers. Indeed, the primary reason for the interstate highway program was to help facilitate daily movement from the cities where most people still worked, to the suburbs, where large numbers were beginning to live. But of course, it was only whites who could live there in most cases. Blacks were still subject to regular discrimination in housing (indeed, most types of housing bias weren't even illegal until 1968), and had been largely unable to take advantage of the government's FHA and VA home loans for the first 30 years of their existence, thanks to racially discriminatory lending criteria built into this government program.

So while nearly 40 percent of white mortgages were being written on the extremely favorable FHA and VA terms by the early 1960s, (making home ownership possible for some 15-20 million white families who wouldn't have otherwise been able to own their own place), virtually no blacks had access to this form of economic opportunity. To then tear down black neighborhoods so as to build highways that would help whites get to their new and growing communities (like Bill O'Reilly's boyhood Levittown), was an especially "pernicious and racist combination of anti-black neglect and white racial preference."

Beyond housing issues, even regular "welfare" receipt is something predicated on history, specifically the history of low-wage employment and inadequate job opportunities, particularly in urban centers. One study from Harlem in the 1990s, found that for every job opening in the area, there were as many as fourteen people looking for work. Nationally, data has long suggested that there are between 7-10 people out of work at any given time, for every above-poverty wage job opening. In other words, there is not enough opportunity in the modern American economy, irrespective of the claims made by conservatives and believed by millions.

In fact, it has long been the official monetary policy of the United States, under the leadership of the Federal Reserve, to raise interest rates whenever unemployment drops "too low," and suddenly the nation is faced with having too many people working. The fear is that too many people working will tighten the labor market, thereby pushing up wages, and then causing a spike in prices, to the detriment of economic well being. By raising the cost of borrowing money, the Fed hopes to cool off business expansion (and thus any attendant and related hiring sprees), and thereby, hold inflation in check.

Putting aside the validity (or lack thereof) of this particular theory, the result of such thinking should be obvious, especially when it is regularly employed to maintain unemployment at around four percent by raising interest rates whenever joblessness drops below that level. Namely, it means that millions of people will be out of work at any given time, not because they are lazy, and certainly not because government handouts appear so luxurious to them, but rather, because it is desired by the government and the nation's economic policymakers that they be out of work.

Indeed, since the official unemployment rate fails to count all who are jobless, such as those who have grown so discouraged by their prospects that they've simply stopped looking (or those who are near jobless, able to pull down only a few hours of work each week, but who are still considered fully employed for the sake of the data), administering monetary policy this way results in as many as 10-12 million people being out of work or seriously underemployed at any given time. They and their dependents will then be (surprise, surprise) poor, and require some type of assistance so as to survive. None of this is a reflection on the values of the poor themselves, though it speaks volumes about the values of the rich who have supported this kind of policy for decades.

But of course, in a media culture incapable of looking deeper than the next 30-second, 100-word sound bite, none of this matters. Indeed, most reporters, news anchors, or journalists of any stripe would be unlikely to even know any of this in the first place. All that matters is the here and now. There's no need for context, background, or history. So, they give us poor people, stealing from stores, careless, penniless and homeless. How they became poor and why they stayed that way doesn't matter, apparently. And by remaining silent on that issue, the mainstream press leaves venal ideologues to fill in the blanks, for an eager public all too willing to believe the worst about people who, for the most part, none of them have ever met.

Thus do we repeatedly plant the seeds for each new round of victim blaming, poor-folks bashing and racism, all the while thinking that just because Anderson Cooper cried on camera and

Fox momentarily turned on Bush (but only for a nanosecond), the Earth's center of gravity moved.

In fact, just as with the aftermath of 9/11, and quite contrary to conventional wisdom, nothing at all has changed.

In today's media, African-Americans, Latinos, Asian-Americans, and Native Americans either are treated as invisible or the source of a particular problem: crime, immigration, the economy. Much of this coverage is documented in a San Francisco State University study that dissected how these stereotypes are perpetuated in photos, headlines, and news footage. These derogatory images are so ingrained in the minds of those who deliver Americans their news that most news people fail to realize how out of touch the media are in reflecting the community they serve.

No one wants to be called a racist. When you ask people why they think African-Americans are on a crime spree, Latinos are flooding the country with drugs, or Asian-Americans are banding together to put "real Americans"—read whites—out of business, they will immediately tell you they saw it on the local news or read it in a newspaper.

So, what's the answer? The more than 5,000 minority journalists at a conference in Atlanta said the solution is to increase racial and ethnic minorities in news management ranks so that those who report, edit, and decide what goes on in the media are proportionately representative of the public at large.

The numbers of minorities in the media industry have increased from four percent to more than 18% in recent years, but the Unity participants believe that rate isn't fast enough. Certainly, they are right. It is unconscionable that the men and few women who manage the media continue to do so without the benefit of enough input from racial and ethnic minorities to make a difference. However, that is not the whole picture. What is seldom discussed is that when minorities get into positions of power—when they become the ones to select, report, and edit the news—they frequently fail to bring multicultural sensitivity to the newsroom and assume the status quo management way of thinking. By the time most minority journalists become an effective part of the management team, they, like almost everyone else around them, have pretty much left their ethnic, racial, and economic roots behind. Their interests are more in line with traditional white upper-middle-class concerns than with the great bulk of minorities who struggle below the poverty level.

There is little if any difference in listening to a member of the media who is a Caucasian, African-American, Latino, Asian-American, or Native American earning a good salary and living a lifestyle that 95% of Americans covet. Once at a certain economic and social level, they begin to complain about welfare abuse, how they're afraid to walk the streets at night, the high cost of buying a home, their kid's college education, and how the plumber, electrician, and cleaning woman ripped them off.

By the time minority journalists make it, most of their racial and ethnic sensitivity may have been ground away by the same middle-class values enjoyed by people of any race or ethnicity who have made it. You don't often cover stories about people and events you don't know about or want to know about. You don't usually put stories in the news that are of no interest to you and your friends. And for all this country's talk about racial and ethnic differences, the number-one difference that separates most people is economic.

It is absolutely essential that American media diversify and integrate racial and ethnic minorities, if for no altruist reason, at least for survival. By the 21st century, most of their viewers and listeners will not be white, but a dazzling array of multicultural people of color. Having more and more representatives of various cultures and backgrounds in the news media can only result in more sensitive, accurate coverage of people and events in a more balanced spectrum of the racial and ethnic minorities that make up the bulk of American citizens.

Don't expect miracles, though. The more human beings achieve money and status, the more they are interested in the status quo and their immediate future and the less they are interested in the grueling problems of poverty and other racial-ethnic concerns. It turns out we are, after all, pretty much alike, even when it comes to caring about those who are less fortunate than we are.

The challenge is the maintaining a constant vigil of the media to insure the accurate characterization of African Americans and others in society when reporting the NEWS. We will no longer permit the media to feature African Americans as their Media Niggah . . .

8

THE CHURCH'S ROLE

Recently, I had an opportunity to visit an ordination service at a local church. The church was in an economically-challenged area of the county where I live. The ordination produced a large turnout, and it was easy for me to get a sense of the economic wellbeing of the congregation. This particular service was mostly comprised of single females, with several small kids. As we waited for the services to begin, I could sense the congregation's anticipation for a comforting word. But the Pastor had not yet arrived, so I went outside for a bit of fresh air. As is normal, I watched the Pastor pull his silver Rolls Royce into his reserved parking space. I was immediately offended. I was further infuriated when I learned that the second parking space belonged to his wife, who drove a tan Rolls Royce. How could they deserve such opulence in the midst of such poverty?

The church failed the community that it is supposed to serve—especially when all do not benefit equally. Where are the programs that are faith-based and designed to uplift the community? I question if God intended for his messengers to benefit more than his congregation?

In some neighborhoods, the churches are the only social service institutions available. And those churches, mostly African-American, are the only thing holding the fraying strands of the community together. Some churches do, in fact, fulfill its role in uplifting the community. Well-renowned Pastor T.D. Jakes commented on this fact in a recent commentary for CNN. The following is what he had to say:

> *"Overcoming many of the existing challenges African-Americans face can be achieved with a plan that encourages a more cohesive community relationship and the spawning of entrepreneurial endeavors and business initiatives, including investments and a thoroughly considered community development initiative.*

> *Many people share these concerns and as a Christian leader committed to the equality of all people and the betterment of people of color, I believe that from the most secluded country church to the largest mega-church, the black church as a corporate body has and will play a vital role in the attainment of these aspirations.*

> *Though the black community was served well by ministers who doubled as political leaders in an era when the pulpit was often our only podium, today, and the African-American community is no longer limited to the pulpit as our primary lecture post. We now have thousands of African-American politicians elected to serve our interests, nonprofit leaders funded to lead our communal efforts and academics educated to research our options, and convey their findings to the world.*

> *Throughout our history, various voices have served our communities well simultaneously. Booker T. Washington shared the public spotlight with W.E.B. DuBois. Ida B. Wells worked against the lynching of black men, while Mary Church Terrell*

worked on behalf of black women. Martin Luther King Jr.'s voice calling for nonviolent integration echoed alongside that of Malcolm X demanding freedom to do for self by any means necessary. As it is in all American communities, no one person or perspective speaks for all African-Americans.

In the final analysis, no singular approach will end America's most pressing problems. Rather, a multiple approach that includes direct assistance, personal empowerment lessons and self-help initiatives as well as speeches, marches and organized resistance will help to dismantle the political and civic structures working against us. We are better together than we are apart."

Aside from Pastor Jakes' commentary, other pastors share in the idea of churches working to benefit the neighborhood by providing resources and much needed services such as day care centers, soup kitchens and substance abuse counseling centers. This is seen in the heart of the Martin Luther King Jr. historical district in Atlanta. Within this district lies Auburn Avenue, home of the civil rights struggle, a rich black business legacy and Sunday morning sermons at some of the largest African American congregations south of the Mason Dixon line. A quarter-block stretch of the avenue is lined on both sides by Wheat Street Plaza North and South and its two strip malls that house 10 small businesses.

What makes these malls significant is that they are the product of the Wheat Street Charitable Foundation, the nonprofit organization that serves as the development arm of Wheat Street Baptist Church. All the shop owners in the malls are members of the church and most of the businesses are black-owned. Four of the merchants have been in the mall since it was built over 25 years ago.

Wheat Street has known for some time what many black churches across the country are quickly discovering: they can be catalysts for the creation of black businesses, jobs and wealth in African American communities. Currently, the Wheat Street church, which doesn't own any of the businesses, clears more than $50,000 annually in rent. But business manager, Eugene Jackson explains that it's not all about creating money for the church. He states that their "mission is about creating economic opportunities for the people in our community."

This brand of Christian capitalism encourages African Americans to pool their dollars to invest in each other and their communities. Unlike a corporation that keeps its profits, church-based business enterprises income thriving businesses, property values of neighboring homes increase. In turn, this attracts more affluent residents and other businesses, which are more likely to take an active role in improving quality-of-life issues; such as safety and adequate education. At its best, the cycle of inner-city poverty is reversed, creating a foundation for economic empowerment.

THE FRUITS OF GOOD WORKS

The 2,000-member congregation also has a 1,000-member credit union with over $1 million in assets. "By belonging to a credit union, you are paying yourself first because you are saving and growing what you earn," says Ben Logan, a 52-year-old accountant who has been a church member for 40 years. "Besides, if you go to a commercial bank, you're nothing but a customer. If you join a credit union, you become an owner and share in the proceeds through interest dividends."

The credit union concept is the foundation of wealth building in the black community. It is the center for educating and guiding those who are unaware of how wealth is built in this country. I have always held the belief that, on bible study night, half of the evening should be devoted to God's teachings, and the other half should be devoted to personal financial management. The credit union concept is a perfect fit for medium to mega churches.

Helping the uninformed understand why Payday loans are a bad idea. Teaching people how to pay themselves first, through credit union savings, is beneficial to their family and really smart, should be the responsibility of the church.

The local community church is also the perfect vehicle for a periodic dialog between adults and adolescent kids. Planned breakfast, with an open conversation format, would give kids an opportunity to discuss their issues with an adult. Such gathering would also be a perfect teaching moment. Boys, without fathers, would have an opportunity benefit from the guidance of adult males, as would girls from adult females. "It takes a community to raise a child."

9

SUMMARY

April 1968 the death of Dr. Martin Luther King started black folk in America on a journey to find the Promise Land. After 300 years of slavery and all the misery, indignation, and deprivation that supported slavery, we embarked on that forty year journey. Some understood that there would be long hard days ahead. They understood that there were behaviors, mental programming, and deficient educational preparation that would have to be eliminated before we entered the Promise Land. And so we wandered.

During that time; we fought with the idol (drugs) worshipers; the propagandists (media); and the power structure (money and politics) to prepare to begin building a productive society once we entered. Very few people realized that the basic infrastructure was in place to build a society of which to be proud of once we entered the promised land.

The first notable change is the emergence of the new Elders (new young leadership) to take on the responsibility for developing the next generations. These people would be known as the Obama generation.

The educational system in this country has failed Black Americans, especially the Black male. The impact of this failure is felt in three areas: family stability, a lack of employment skills necessary to financially support a family, lack of social skills necessary to be that source of pride for his family, and finally in limiting the ability to effectively communicate. We are complicit in the failure of the educational system by not exercising our rights not to support failing system, and by not exercising our right of educational choice. We can now move our kids out of bad public schools using the voucher system available to us, to other productive options such as: Charter Schools, Religious Schools, and Private Schools. If Black kids continue to fail, we must look to ourselves to blame.

Over the past forty years, contrary to media propaganda, a clear understanding of the importance of education has increased the focus on developing alternative school systems. Now educational options like charter schools, voucher programs, military academies, and gender based alternatives are being developed.

Post high school career paths are part of the new curriculum, for example; vocational educational skills development; IT and other technical programs are seriously under consideration; and finally, school to career union apprentice programs are slowly being structured.

Strong emphasis will always drive Advance Placement preparation. Post high school education is always the desired path. Some will not be able to exercise that option upon graduation, so the school to work option should be available.

Historically Black Colleges and Universities (HBCU)s are a under utilized national treasure for black kids. The problem is that in some instances they sometimes lack proper management and necessary funding to competitively prepare black students for the market .

place. This can be fixed. This must be fixed to provide black students a black educational option—their option for an education in a nurturing environment that is black centric. But first, these schools must be developed as a resource. Our resource . . . .

Give a man a fish and he can feed himself for a day. Teach him to fish and he can feed himself for a life time."

African Americans have allowed themselves to be defined by the media as national economic dependents. Nothing is farther from the truth. We have a spending resource larger than most countries in the world. We had earned income (GDP) of 1 Trillion dollars in 2013. By comparison, that is larger than the GDP of Argentina 483.5 billion, South Africa 491.4 billion, and Poland with 463 billion. The problem is not how much we have. The problem is how we use it. We tend to spend our wealth on disposable items. We aren't poor. We are just "bling-bling broke," and until we understand and appreciate the value of our financial resources, we will always lag behind in the quest for real wealth in America.

Wealth building is the next most important element in the development of a proud, strong black segment of this American society. We have the wealth, it's just not focused. I used the term Bling-Bling broke to explain the value that we some times placed on black wealth. *I have since come to realize that the new elders are becoming major players in this country. They are starting to buy shares in the wealth produced in this country. They are developing a new value system that will not leave them Bling-Bling broke.*

Jay-Z (Hip Hop mogul) for example, own a share in a NBA team. Tyler Perry owns a movie studio, and Oprah owns everything. The new elders have started to become sophisticated in the amassing and managing wealth. They now have the dignity that wealth bring. They understand the value of their money. It is time for the rest of black society to understand the power of their money. It time to understand that wealth brings dignity.

The media has been allowed to define who African Americans are. Therefore, we are what the media has portrayed us to be. Their vision was never more obvious than the depiction of blacks during the Katrina disaster. Every image that the world saw was of black people that were looting, murdering, drug dealing, welfare stealing, and refugees. The same images were played over and over, with little attempt to validate the stories. It wasn't until Jesse Jackson chastised Campbell Brown, of NBC News, on air, that those black folk were displaced, not refugees, did the constant references stop. This depiction was not a Katrina anomaly. Instead, it was standard industry practice. We have never protested loud enough or long enough for it to stop and until we exercise our economic free choice by not tuning into those stations who continue to define us in that undeserved negative way, will this practice stop.

Control the politics in America, and you will control your fate, a lesson that Black Americans have began to learn. We are far more loyal to the Democratic Party than we are to ourselves. We have made our vote valueless because Republicans don't need us to win; and Democrats don't want us until they need us to win. We, on the other hand, will always follow anyone who will promise us civil rights. How sad? We are the only ethnic group that has come to depend on someone to lead us, to articulate our dreams, and negotiate with White folk for our rights. We fail to remember how potent we almost became as a political force when Jesse Jackson ran for President. The political establishment was fearful that 12 million blacks would vote as a block, instead of voting in lockstep with the Democrats. I never understood why Jesse Jackson did not continue to lead us as the powerful voting block that we had become, instead he lead us back to the Democrats. We must learn to set the agenda of our representatives, not the reverse. So far, our so called leadership has only succeeded in leading us off a cliff. That's not their fault, it is ours.

Lastly, political power, the vote in America is political power. In 2008 African Americans elected a president, a black president, Barack Obama. Such was unimaginable at any other time in history. Yet by unity of effort, we saw our dreams—no Martin Luther King's dream realized. It took unity of purpose and a dream. Therefore we must never become complacent—whites will take back your dignity, your wealth, and your dream, as they did after the Civil War.

Tell Martin that we fulfilled his dream—we got to the Promised Land. Now we must begin to build that shining city on the hill, the city that we can all be proud of Our Shining City on the Hill.

NOTES

CHAPTER 1

1. *"The Willie Lynch Legacy,"* ProQuest Information & Learning Company, September/October 1999.
2. Clay, W. (1993). *"Just Permanent Interests."*
3. Smith, P. (2002) *"Trial by Fire: A People's History of the Civil War and Reconstruction."*

CHAPTER 2

1. Jones, J. (2006). *"Marriage is for White People."*
2. Burnett, J. (2006). *"It's Not What Bill Cosby Said—It's the Reaction To It."*
3. Mitchell, M. (2004). *"Hey, Hey, Hey! Cosby Needs to Ease Up On Poor Blacks."*
4. Jolma, C. (2002). *Insight.*

CHAPTER 3

1. Davis, L.E. (2003, July). *"In explaining why African-American boys lag behind in school—and deciding what to do about it."*
2. Lord, M. (2003, August). *"Freedom of choice: parents frustrated with conventional public schools are bucking the system. Here Black mothers who chose education alternatives share their success stories."*

3. *"Charter Schools,"* GNU Free Documentation License. Available Online:
4. Heaney, J. (1999, May). *"Easy Pickings—Effects of Teacher Tenure."*
5. Caldwell, L., Baldwin, Walls, C.K. & Smith, T. (2004). *"Preliminary Effects of a Leisure Education Program to Promote Healthy Use of Free Time Among Middle School Adolescents."*

CHAPTER 4

1. Stephens, B. (1997). *Talking Dollars and Making Sense: A Wealth Building Guide for African Americans.*
2. (1995). Dept. of Commerce Economics and Statistics, Bureau of Census.
3. (1996). Dept. of Commerce Economics and Statistics, Bureau of Census, Black Owned Businesses Strongest in Years.
4. (2001). Dept. of Commerce Economics and Statistics, Bureau of Census, Update on Country's African American Population.
5. *"Staying Ahead of the Pack."* (2001).
6. *The African American Market.* (2003).
7. Singletary, M. (2006, February). "Keys to Black Empowerment."

CHAPTER 5

1. Mosley, W. (2006, February). *"A New Black Power."*
2. Coulter, A. (2004, November). *"Democrats Losing Grip on Most Loyal Vote."*
3. Ponnuru, R. & Nadler, R. (2001, March). *"The Simplest Outreach."*
4. Jones, J. (1997, February). *Black Enterprise.*

CHAPTER 6

1. (2001). Entertainment Television & Hot 103 Jamz.
2. Saltzman, J. (1994, November). *"In Whose Image?—Media Stereotypes of Minorities."*
3. Bonner, F.A. (2006). *"Wade in the Water: A Contemporary Metaphor."*

CHAPTER 7

1. Jakes, T.D. (2006, July). *"No Political Party Can Contain Us."* CNN.

Foot Notes

1. Harlem's Man with the Plan By <u>Paul Tough</u>
   Photograph of J. Seward Johnson, Jr.'s "The Awakening" located Hains Point, Washington D.C. Photographer

   Introduction
   Speech by Martin Luther King in Memphis, Tenn. April 3, 1998

Chapter 1

1. Excerpts from Ordinary Children, Extraordinary Teachers and Marva Collins' Way.
2. Ibid
3. Ibid
4. Ibid
   Paul Tough <u>January/February 2009 Issue</u>
5. What Ever it Takes
6. Ibid
7. Ibid
8. Kathy Piechura-Couture, Stetson University
9. Ibid
10. Ibid
11. Ibid
12. Ibid
13. Ibid
14. Ibid
15. Ibd
16. Ibid
17. Ibid

18. Ibid
19. Ibid
20. Ibid
21. Ten-hut! Are public military high schools good for teens?
Nov 12, 2007
COPYRIGHT 2007 Weekly Reader Corp.
22 Ibid
23 Ibid
24 Ibid
25 Ibid
26 Ibid
27 Ibid
28 Ibid
29 Ibid
30 Ibid
31 Ibid
32 Ibid
33 California Department of Education
After School Learning and Safe Neighborhoods Partnerships Program
released in 2002
34 Ibid
35 Ibid
36 Ibid
37 Ibid
38 Ibid
39 Ibid
40 Ibid
41 Ibid
42 Ibid
43 Ibid
44 Ibid

The Bill & Melinda Gates Foundation
Redefining the American High School—The Facts

[2]   Ibid.

[3]   Carey, Kevin, "Choosing to Improve: Voices from Colleges and Universities with Better Graduation Rates," Washington, DC: Achieve, 2005. No source cited.

[4]   Peter D. Hart Research Associates, "Rising to the Challenge: Are High School Graduates Prepared for College and Work," Washington, DC: Achieve, 2005.

[5]   American Diploma Project, "Ready Or Not: Creating a High School Diploma That Works," Washington, DC: Achieve, Inc, 2004.

[6]   Johnson J. and Duffet, A., "Where We Are Now: 12 Things You Need to Know About Public Opinion and Public Schools," NY: Public Agenda, 2002. Reality Check.

[7]   Carnevale, Anthony and Desrochers, Donna, "Standards for What? The Economic Roots of K-16 Reform," Washington, DC: Educational Testing Service, 2004.

[8]   Sum, Andrew; Khatiwada, Ishwar; Pond, Nathan; and Trub'skyy, Mykhaylo, "Left Behind in the Labor Market: Labor Market Problems of the Nation's Out-of-School, Young Adult Populations," prepared for the Alternative Schools Network, Boston: Center for Labor Market Studies, Northeastern University, 2002.

[9]   National Center for Education Statistics, "Remedial Education at Degree-Granting Postsecondary Institutions in Fall 2000," Washington, DC: U.S. Department of Education, 2003.

[10]   Carnevale and Desrochers, 2004.

[11]   Baum, Sandy and Payea, Kathleen, "Education Pays: The Benefits of Higher Education for Individuals and Society," NJ: College Board, 2004.

3.   Explaining why African-American boys lag in school—and deciding what to do about it
      Tuesday, July 29, 2003
      By Larry E. Davis

4.   What is a historically black college/university (HBCU)? 8/27/2008
      By Liz Funk Provided by: Next Step Magazine

Chapter 2

1. *School-to-Career*
   A QUICK GUIDE for Organized Labor
2. 25 Highest-Paying Jobs for High School Grads
   HR.BLR.com's Salary Center

Chapter 3

1. List of Wealthiest African-Americans
   From Wikipedia, the free encyclopedia Retrieved from *http://*
   en.wikipedia.org/wiki/List_of_Wealthiest_African-Americans"
2. *Cathy Mickens of Neighborhood Housing Services in Jamaica, Queens.*
3. *Ibid*
4. *Boston College Center on Wealth and Philanthropy (CWP) projects(April*
   18, 2005
5. *Ibid*
6. Warmed-over Myths of Black Wealth
7. Ibid
8. Newsflash from CNBC's NEWBOs: If you're black and can't rap or
   play ball, forget about making it in America.
   By *Alfred Edmond, Jr.*—February 27, 2009
9. Ibid
10. Ibid

Chapter 4

1. Do Democrats need the black vote?
   By Robert Schlesinger
   April 4, 2008 . . . 12:02 pm
2. ibid

Chapter 5

1.   Black Fraternities Thrive, Often on Adversity
     By ISABEL WILKERSON
     Published: Monday, October 2, 1989
2.   *The Connecticut Coalition for Achievement NOW*